Our Story

For the next generation

Ashton, Maquah, Winston^H, Tayamni, Chetan, Alexa, Elizabetta, Winston^N, K'nek'nek, Repoy, and Theodore

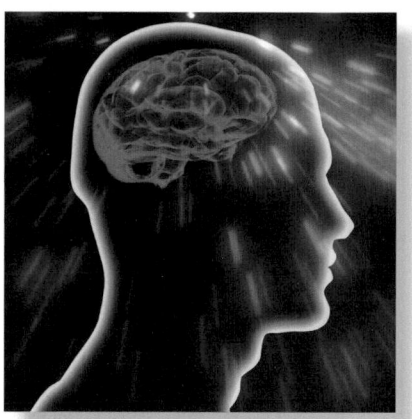

OurStory

How Cultures Shaped People to Get Things Done

W. Penn Handwerker

Routledge
Taylor & Francis Group

LONDON AND NEW YORK

First published 2015 by Left Coast Press, Inc.

Published 2016 by Routledge
2 Park Square, Milton Park, Abingdon, Oxon OX14 4RN
711 Third Avenue, New York, NY 10017, USA

Routledge is an imprint of the Taylor & Francis Group, an informa business

Copyright © 2015 Taylor & Francis

All rights reserved. No part of this book may be reprinted or reproduced or utilised in any form or by any electronic, mechanical, or other means, now known or hereafter invented, including photocopying and recording, or in any information storage or retrieval system, without permission in writing from the publishers.

Notice:
Product or corporate names may be trademarks or registered trademarks, and are used only for identification and explanation without intent to infringe.

Library of Congress Cataloging-in-Publication Data:
Handwerker, W. Penn.
 Our story : how cultures shaped people to get things done / W. Penn Handwerker.
     pages cm
 Includes bibliographical references and index.
 ISBN 978-1-59874-677-8 (hardback) -- ISBN 978-1-59874-678-5 (paperback) -- ISBN 978-1-59874-679-2 (institutional ebook)
 1. Culture--Origin. 2. Social evolution. I. Title.
 GN357.5.H363 2015
 306--dc23
                    2014032134

ISBN 978-1-59874-678-5 paperback
ISBN 978-1-59874-677-8 hardback

Contents

Acknowledgments and Special Recognition   *7*

Introduction: Still Looking After All These Years ~ 150 Years! Drives You Crazy   *9*

Part I   On Cultures

Chapter 1   Cultures Originate in Intelligent Minds   23

Chapter 2   Cultures Establish Moral Visions   34

Chapter 3   Morally Ordered Behavior Gives Cultures Agency   46

Chapter 4   Living Requires Many Cultures; Thriving Requires They Be Well-Designed   60

Part II   On the Properties of Mind That Produce Agency

Chapter 5   Coercive Force Yields Morally Ordered Behavior   71

Chapter 6   Cognitive Coercion May Kill You Before You Get Anywhere   81

Chapter 7   Intelligence Makes for Disturbing Irony   91

Lessons Learned   Cultures Aren't Merely Curiosities and How "Others" Think and Act   109

References   *121*

Index   *127*

About the Author   *128*

Acknowledgments and Special Recognition

Homer Barnett and Clifford Geertz—for pointing out that cultures come from our minds;

Marvin Harris—for reminding me that humans cannot survive, much less evolve, unless they act;

W. P. Handwerker II and Joe Jorgensen—for illustrating the inseparability of truth and integrity and evidence;

Rose Jones, Catherine Fuentes, and Richard Wilson—for the challenge to precisely describe how cultures exercise coercive force;

Roy D'Andrade—for helping me to see that the former counted as an important challenge and for the language to both describe cultures more precisely and see more clearly how they work;

Russ Bernard—for pointing out key issues I left out the first time through; and

Willamette University c. 1962–1966, particularly Drs. Baker (English), Stillings (Political Science), Paulin (Art History), Rademaker (Sociology), and Tod Mikuriya (Oregon State Hospital), for insisting on truth-seeking through critical analysis of evidence, calling my attention to the issues addressed in this book, and challenging me to put the pieces together.

Introduction

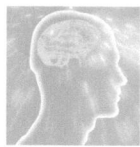

Still Looking After All These Years ~150 Years! Drives You Crazy

Adam Smith's *The Wealth of Nations* (1776) nicely rationalized what we know intuitively, that flourishing lives come from conscious, rational decisions.

We now know that this intuition is pure fantasy, told to us by an integral part of our brain that tells stories. We reason, certainly, but biases make it impossible to make a rational choice. Consciousness of which choice we made occurs after the fact. Ordinarily, moreover, we remain blissfully ignorant of the biases that direct the course of our lives.

True, rational choice theories provide powerful explanations in the social and behavioral sciences. These theories assume that the weighted average of preferences and the likelihood of their realization explain why people choose one thing over another. Real-world choices, however, depend heavily on availability heuristics, confirmation biases, evaluations based on likeness rather than likelihood, overestimates of the likelihood of rare events, and many forms of "irrelevant" information. If, for example, we frame a choice as a loss, we discount real risks; if we frame a choice as a gain, we exaggerate the same risks. Not only do real-world choices exhibit predictable "irrationalities," rational choice theories cannot explain preference. Bueno de Mesquita's rational choice model, for example, achieves remarkably accurate predictions, but these depend on accurate empirical knowledge of decision-maker preferences, not a theory of preferences. Consequently, rational choice deterrence theories, which start from the familiar premise that strength deters violence and weakness elicits it, inconsistently identify deterrents and do not tell us what makes a threat credible. Empirical tests thus may provide only ambiguous support, and policies based on these theories rarely (if ever) work well

How, then, have we thrived? It took ~99,800 of the last 100,000 years to produce a human population of 1 billion. But we added 6 billion more in just 200 years. If we can't make conscious, rational decisions, how is this increase possible?

Simple. Human minds contain a set of coevolved mental mechanisms that work together to make it so. First, our minds produce imaginary things—speculative postulates that come out of our consciousness in the form a story told by what Michael Gazzaniga called our mind's Interpreter. If the story applies to the world around us, its implications tell us what we should expect of that world—for example, that the sun rises in the morning and sets in the evening, that living things depend on cells for their construction and operation, and that things that do nothing deteriorate and fall apart. If our Interpreter spins a story that applies to human agency, we call its implications *cultural norms*. These implications tell us what we should expect from the people we live among and expresses those expectations in a moral vision about what's right and what's not and how to respond to norm violations; for example, you should respect your parents and love your children and go to class on time.

The adaptive value of these cognitive mechanisms depends on the coevolution of a set of cognitive biases to reduce innovation-induced uncertainty, give emotional weights to experiences to differentiate opportunities from threats, and imbue shared moral visions with the power to force compliance with that vision. This set of cognitive biases yields codependencies that produce the teamwork that, for specific behavioral domains, we call *cultures*. Whereas individuals break easily, teams don't, and they achieve goals that individuals find elusive. Finally, evolved-choice frames give agency to individuals to try new ways when old ways yield dangerous effects. The outcome? A culture-creating and culture-dependent creature with a mind that generates a continual flow of innovations and uncertainties and depends for its well-being on cooperation with other like creatures. Hence, our preferences.

What's the Point?

This book tells the story about how innovations in human minds created cultures and why the effects of cultures produced increasingly intense selection for the complementary cognitive mechanisms (like language and a whole host of cognitive biases that include wishful thinking, the confirmatory bias, learned helplessness, closure, heuristics, and choice frames) that were required to coevolve with intelligence to make cultures work effectively. Along the way, it explains the origins of morality, how and under which conditions we help or kill our neighbor or family member, and it provides some hints about how we may resolve conflict, minimize violence, and heal from the traumatic stress that will otherwise kill us.

This story's central finding? That nothing happens unless there's a culture to do it. Pick a goal: getting married, creating a secure retirement, putting food on your (literal or figurative) table, or receiving a bachelor's degree. World peace doesn't exist because we haven't yet created a culture to produce it. Or how about more esoteric goals, like gay men's dependence on a culture to become gay. Doubtful? Read David Halperin's new (2012) book *How to Be Gay*.

Recognition of the power of cultures has become widespread. Here's a very short list of recent books about cultures and their effects:

- *Change the Culture, Change the Game* (2011), Roger Connors and Tom Smith
- *The Clash of the Cultures: Investment vs. Speculation* (2012), John C. Bogle
- *A New Culture of Learning* (2011), Douglas Thomas and John Seely Brown
- *Broken Promises* (2011), Edward C. Green
- *Carnage and Culture* (2001), Victor Davis Hanson
- *The Other Wes Moore: One Name, Two Fates* (2010), Wes Moore
- *Life at the Bottom: The Worldview That Makes the Underclass* (2001), Theodore Dalrymple

Whatever you wish to accomplish, you'll fail unless you participate in the right culture (or set of cultures). This may entail switching cultures or creating a new one, if an appropriate culture doesn't already exist. This concept applies, too, to all people, others as well as you. Global problems of all kinds— fighting, maiming, and killing of many kinds, health disparities, racism, drugs, poverty, and the environment, to name a few—originate in clashing cultural assumptions. The high incidence of rape on U.S. college campuses, for example, reflects conflict between cultural postulates bearing on which rights are unalienable and which are not and what counts as a sexual invitation. Prevailing arguments frame the problem correctly as conflict but wrongly as conflicts between individual agents (whether people, organizations, or countries). Because cultures act as coercive agents, individuals cannot change unless they *shift cultures or create a new one*. Effective resolutions thus depend on understanding the cultural foundations of conflict, how human minds create cultures and imbue them with the coercive force, and the circumstances in which individual agency forces a shift from one culture to another or creates a new one.

What Are These Things, Cultures?

Much confusion surrounds the idea of culture. We see this as ambiguity and incomplete explanation in books like those listed above that explore the power of a culture. Edward B. Tylor gave us the first modern definition of what we call cultures in his 1871 book *Primitive Culture*. Tylor argued that cultures consist of stuff we learn from the people we live with that exhibit holistic, integrated properties. For Tylor, culture isn't just art, or families, or ways of making a living, or religion. Culture is all these. Culture is more than all these because the things that constitute it fit together. Change one part of a culture and you'll change other parts.

We've come to understand, however, that evolved properties of our mind tell us what to learn. Recognition that we can no longer distinguish meaningfully between learned and instinctive behavior set off a search for evolved specific neural architectures, or modules, that regulate human behavior. Evolutionary psychologists drew the conclusion that patterns of behavior emerged from a large number of built-in modes of mental processing. There's one for language learning, another for cheating detection, and others for mate selection, for different kinds of social attachments, and for all the other important domains of human activity. Jointly, these mental modules produce ecologically adaptive behavior for individuals.

This postulate ignores the commonplace observation that we learn nearly everything we know from other people. Ralph Linton made this point vividly in his 1936 book *The Study of Man*. He tells us how an ordinary American citizen, who dresses in clothes modeled after garments created by nomads of the Central Asian steppes, begins his day. He eats for breakfast a version of cereal and milk, a practice that originated in Southwest Asia and, perhaps, an egg from a species of bird domesticated in Southeast Asia together with strips of flesh from an animal domesticated in East Asia that had been salted and smoked by a process developed in northern Europe. Linton ends his commentary about how we transform into the banal components of our personal lives what originated as cultural curiosities from far-flung places and long-ago times— "cultural appropriation" according to some people, "diffusion" or "borrowing" to others— with this statement:

> When our friend has finished eating he settles back to smoke, an American Indian habit, consuming a plant domesticated in Brazil in either a pipe, derived from the Indians of Virginia, or a cigarette, derived from Mexico. If he is hearty enough he may even attempt a cigar, transmitted to use from the Antilles by way of Spain. While smoking he reads the news of the day, imprinted in characters invented by the ancient Semites upon a material invented in China by a process invented in Germany. As he absorbs the accounts of foreign troubles he will, if he is a good conservative citizen, thank a Hebrew deity in an Indo-European language that he is 100% American. (1936: 327)

Domain-specific mental modules probably exist and, in one sense, it's probably true that "our skulls house a stone-aged mind" that produces adaptive behavior. Because individuals break easily, this can't be all the story. It can't even be a significant part of it. We thrive only when and to the extent that we coordinate our behavior with that of other people. Three well documented (and more general) mechanisms—intelligence, cognitive biases, and choice frames—allow us to see how minds take environmental information and turn them into things with agency.

Where Does One Culture End and Another One Start?

In the late 20th century, work by Jim Boster, Kim Romney, and others improved Tylor's model in ways that finally allowed us to say definitively where one culture ends and another begins. Since Tylor's time, we've taken for granted that groups "have" one. Americans have a culture. Alaskan Eskimos have a culture. The Kru who live on the coast of West Africa have a culture. We've done so by assumption, however—not evidence. We've also dismissed, downplayed, or overlooked cultural variation within the groups that (we supposed) have a culture. Romney's model helped us realize that "groups" may or may not share beliefs, value, norms, customs, habits, or rules. Characteristically, the groups we think of as having a culture correspond only with a social label. And social labels come and go. On the Pepper Coast of West Africa, as I've pointed out occasionally, men who differentiated themselves as father and son became undifferentiated members of a regional political group called a *dako* that competed with its neighbors for control over land, rights over women and children, and trade; men of competing *dako* became undifferentiated *Kru* when they sought work on ships plying the commercial shipping lanes off the West African coast. A few *Kru*, along with Yoruba and despite marked differences in language, customs, and physical attributes, became undifferentiated slaves who worked plantations in the West Indies and the southern United States. Those who found a way to own their own plantations and slaves came to be called *Gens du Colours* in Haiti and equivalent names elsewhere, although their descendants as well as those of their slaves who now live in the United States became undifferentiated "African Americans."

Accumulating evidence thus tells us that we turned the relationship between cultures and groups on its head. Once we ask the question "Who shares what with whom?" we discover that cultures— specific sets of shared understandings and ways of doing things—identify the group. Some cultural groups correspond with labels like Americans, Eskimo, and Kru. Others correspond with entities—for instance, specific football teams (the Dallas Cowboys), financial institutions (Bank of America), and businesses (Intel Corporation). Some correspond with a group with no name, a culture of higher ed, that spans the globe. Faculty and students at Moscow State, the University of Liberia, the University of Singapore, the Sorbonne, and the University of Connecticut, for example, share an unnamed but easily describable global culture of higher education.

Even today, social scientists commonly assume that differences that show up among samples drawn from differently labelled populations—say, people in the United States, people in Japan, and people in Hong Kong, count as cultural differences. They employ the same comparative method to samples drawn from populations with other labels (say, men and women, old and young, employed or not, or incarcerated or not) but show no awareness that these differences, too, may measure cultural differences. However, irrespective of group label, differences identified by this embarrassingly naive procedure fail to meet the most elementary criteria to warrant a claim of cultural difference—as John Gatewood points out in his paper *Criteria for Regarding Group-Group Differences in Cognition as "Cultural" Differences* (Society for Applied Anthropology & Society for Anthropological Sciences, 2014). Like the normative force that comes from coherency.

What Makes a Culture Coherent?

Romney, as Tylor, however, could not describe the intellectual coherency of cultures. Yes, we can tell who agrees with whom about what and to what degree. Why and how this set goes together? Who knows. The idea that cultural institutions consist of shared sets of rules presents the same dilemma. We still don't have a clue why and how this set of rules differs from any other randomly selected set. Coherence implies nonrandom selection. E. A. Hoebel and Lauriston Sharp solved the coherence conundrum in mid-20th century, although we were too involved in other controversies at the time to see the importance of their observation: namely, cultures rest on speculative postulates about the nature of behavioral realms, and these postulates tell us the moral vision suitable to those realms.

"Higher Ed" consists, for example, of such things as colleges or universities, each of which consists of things like administrations, faculties, facilities, and a student body. Facilities consist of things like classrooms, offices, and dorms. Faculties consist of instructors who come in a variety of names that tell rank (for example, Professor and Assistant Professor) and academic discipline (for instance, anthropology, political science, and biology). Administrations consist of such things as Presidents, Provosts, Deans, and Registrars. Students consist of people who seek a degree in higher education but who come in a variety of names that tell rank (first-year freshman, senior, seventh-year perpetual student) and academic discipline (for instance, engineering and agricultural economics).

The culture also comes with a distinctive set of rules and expectations. These apply whether if a student attends Humboldt State University or the University of Aruba. Students should sign up for classes, pay tuition, and reliably show up for class on time. As a student who goes to class you should (among many other "shoulds"), ordinarily, (a) prepare for the class before arrival, (b) take a seat, (c) take out writing materials with which to take notes, (d) listen carefully to the instructor and the comments or questions of other students, (e) take careful and thorough notes, (f) participate in class discussions, and (g) leave with a clear understanding of the class assignments to complete before the next meeting. Similarly, you should not (a) yell obscenities or (among many other "should nots") (b) jump up on the desk and drop your pants.

During the last half of the 20th century, it became fashionable to restrict the term *culture* to ideas. Behavior, after all, may conflict dramatically with professed beliefs. This narrow focus created a dilemma. As A. R. Radcliffe-Browne famously observed in mid-century, quadratic equations cannot commit murder. Ideas can't defend you from an attack, put food on your table, or produce children, much less carry out the activities that allow those children to survive to adulthood and form their own families. Ideas, Marvin Harris repeatedly observed, can't bear on human survival, much less human thriving, unless they relate to actions. Cultural rules and expectations—call them *cultural norms*— apply to acts. What's the point of linking ideas and acts unless there's something important there?

Cultures as Relative to What?

A related dilemma originated in the observation that the ideas that constitute cultures originated in our imaginations, out of our experience. From this perspective, every culture is the same, just different. Differences reflect variations in experience. There's no reason to think one culture is any better than another, because it makes no sense to say that one set of experiences is better than another.

But moral equivalence didn't square with the idea that cultures provided humans a distinctive means to successfully adapt to environmental variation. Foragers, for example, characteristically live as parts of small, mobile, and egalitarian family-based communities. In Africa, Eurasia, the Middle East, and the New World, non-industrialized farmers, by contrast, characteristically lived as parts of settled communities organized as wealth-based hierarchies. That the effectiveness of a culture varies with the problems it was designed to address makes nonsense of the claim that no culture is better than another.

Winnowing through the variants and errors produced by lots of people over many years reveals increasingly effective solutions to specific problems. The creation and use of the first stone tools would have made it easier to shape digging sticks with which to extract roots, to cut branches with which to build shelters, to kill, carve up, and dismember game, and to protect oneself and one's food from competitors. The later use of fire made it possible to harden wood in ways that created more efficient and durable digging sticks and lances, to occupy colder regions, to cook food, and to protect oneself and one's food from competitors. The ability to harden wood made it possible to kill game more efficiently, and improved stone tool design made it possible to carve up and dismember game more efficiently. The ability to cook food profoundly transformed both the reliability and the quality of the nutritional base of our ancestors. Cooking improved the nutritional value of meat, because it reduced the likelihood of acquiring worms, which would have been common when meat was not cooked before it was eaten. Cooking increased the nutritional quality of the diet by making essential nutrients more readily available. Finally, cooking made it possible for people to use a vast range of new vegetable resources, which, uncooked, had been indigestible or even poisonous. A sense of community and interdependence among people who hunted, cooked, and lived together yielded more effective cooperation and increasingly efficient production, reduced infant, child, and maternal mortality, and more effective defense. Campfires extended the length of time our ancestors could carry out both work and social activities; they also provided a community focus for both, which contributed to the spread of information, enhanced the importance of communication, and quickened winnowing processes. Findings from Qesem Cave in Israel, for example, suggest that our ancestors were highly effective cooperative hunters more than 200,000 years ago. Within the next 100,000 years, however, evidence suggests a more formal division of labor based on competence, as well as significant changes in how food was shared. These differences correspond to the differences between the Lower and Middle Paleolithic, which entailed major changes into who we are today. The Toba supereruption around 74,000 years ago may have reduced the total number of people on the planet to anywhere from 3,000 to 10,000—the size of a small college or university. In doing so, it radically changed what it took to survive, much less thrive. Teamwork gave our ancestors selective advantages millions of years ago, but the change between the Middle and the Upper Paleolithic implies vastly superior teamwork. Within the next 60,000 years we occupied the frozen north, the scalding deserts, 10,000-foot tall mountains, and dense, steamy rainforest. By the end of the Pleistocene, it took only 5,000 years or so to figure out how to successfully evolve from a foraging to a food-producing way of life. Change occurs faster today by many orders of magnitude, but cultural change remains constant.

Problems Force Cultures to Change

Recall Moore's Law, for example. In 1965 Intel cofounder G. E. Moore drew attention to the order of magnitude change rate, anticipated earlier by Alan Turing, that characterized computer technologies. (Moore focused on the number of transistors on integrated circuits, but the law that took his name also applies to memory capacity, processing speed, and pixels in digital cameras.) In 50 years what used to take up a room now fits into a smart phone. I shared results from my first desk calculator with colleagues down the hall. I couldn't get much farther when hand-calculators appeared, although the processing power changed from room-size to desk-size to pocket-size. Now we send computer output nearly instantaneously from nearly any point on the globe to any other. I met Se Wilson my second day in West Africa, in 1968—when few people had telephones and overseas calls were routed through a central telephone exchange. Se still lives in Cape Palmas, Liberia, but we now speak regularly (or text) via cell phone.

The constancy of change corresponds with two behavioral rules—do nothing you don't have to and do everything else you can to improve your life. The constancy of cultural change appears as changes, moreover, in both ideas and action. If cultures comprise both ideas and behavior, the correspondence of norms to behavior shifts from a reason to define cultures as ideas to a critical research issue. Effective adaptations exhibit a close correspondence between cultural norms and patterns of behavior; ineffective adaptations don't. A shift in the correspondence between cultural norms and behavior from close to random signals that a culture has begun to evolve into something new. Change of a cultural assumption wreaks havoc with the moral corollaries of the previous culture. In the early 20th century on Australia's Cape York Peninsula, for example, dramatic falsification of postulates that rationalized much Yir Yoront behavior left confused and demoralized old Yir Yoront men to seek refuge in toothpaste cults. The postulates? Just that old people dominated younger people and men dominated women. Women required axes for much of their work, but axe availability depended on trading activities carried out by older men. Stone axes, a vital tool owned only by older men, came to symbolize the superiority of the old and male over the young and female. The deference and respect given by women to men disappeared quickly, however, after women's dependence on men was broken by the practice of Anglican missionaries to freely distribute steel axes.

Cultures as Things—with Agency

And once we take a fresh look at how cultures may solve problems, we can see how recent work by John Searle and Roy D'Andrade has opened the way to take seriously the early 20th-century arguments by Alfred Kroeber and Leslie White that cultures exhibit the properties of things and truly, not metaphorically, act as agents.

White called culture a thing *sui generis*, meaning that it fit into no other category, that it constituted a thing unique among all that we know—a new order of reality. Kroeber, in a similar vein, pointed out that we don't have to study individual minds to study culture, because it possesses properties that go far beyond individuals, even if individuals are its only repositors. If a specialist dies, that bit of culture goes to the grave with him or her. But most of culture forms the environment into which we arrive as infants, changes independently of how we might want it to change, and requires our attention however much we may detest it. You can't wish culture away, any more than you can wish away the rising and setting of the sun and the phases of the moon. Because culture possesses qualities that go beyond the organisms that create, bear, and change it, Kroeber called culture a *superorganic* phenomenon.

Until recently, however, people who sensed the power of cultures could not explain how cultures—which, as Ward Goodenough pointed out, consisted of nothing more substantive than abstractions produced by ethnographers—exerted coercive force. Cultural explanations remained tautologies. It was obvious, indeed true-by-definition, that culture determined what people thought and did, because if those people had a different culture they would think and act differently.

We escape tautology once we imagine that cultures acquire *sui generis*, superorganic properties because each consists of shared (shared = cultural) assumptions that produce a moral universe of the rules that everyone should live by (cultural norms). When the people who share that moral universe enforce consequences for breaking behavioral rules (cultural norms), they force each other to make choices A, P, and X rather than B, Q, and Y. This situation produces coordinated patterns of behavior (teamwork) that achieves goals, both small scale (we share our food and skills with others) and large scale (the production of a new generation, and another, and another). As Kroeber and White pointed out, cultures thus count as a new level of phenomena, just as organ systems (that consist of a bunch of cells) count as a new level of phenomena. Cultures, consequently, act as agents. Because they force people to do one thing rather than another they promote success or guarantee failure in one behavioral domain or another—or many.

Thinking of cultures as domain specific also allows us to precisely describe how and why they exhibit coherence. Assumptions give cultures coherence. Classroom norms rest on the assumption that you attend class to learn. Everything you should do (for example, take a seat, take notes) helps you to achieve that. Everything you should not do (for instance, dropping your pants) detracts from that.

This conceptual restriction also makes possible precise descriptions of where one culture ends and another begins—cultural differences correspond with differences in assumptions. And because cultures apply to specific behavioral domains, as Edward Sapir hinted in the first half of the 20th century, we live our lives by drawing on and as participants in multiple cultures.

Just to Clarify . . .

Popular culture holds that the most important differences between cultures, and between individuals, consist of differences in values. The abortion debate in the United States contrasts people who place a high value on life, even for unborn children, and people who place a high value on women's ability to make their own life choices. Political conservatives place great value on freedom. Political liberals place great value on . . . freedom.

Wait. That can't be right.

It is right, however. Ask any political conservative or liberal. Values don't differentiate political conservatives and liberals any more than values differentiate "right-to-life" or "right-to-choose" advocates.

Here's why. Values consist of all those things we think of as "good." Values research, particularly the cross-national work carried out by Shalom H. Schwartz and colleagues, has revealed 10 major value categories found throughout the world. Here they are, each with examples of more specific values:

Power: authority; leadership; dominance

Achievement: success; capability; ambition; influence; intelligence; self-respect

Hedonism: pleasure; enjoying life

Stimulation: daring activities; varied life; exciting life

Self-direction: creativity; freedom; independence; curiosity; choosing your own goals

Universalism: broadmindedness; wisdom; social justice; equality; harmony

Benevolence: helpfulness; honesty; forgiveness; loyalty; responsibility; friendship

Tradition: accepting one's portion in life; humility; devoutness; respect for tradition; moderation

Conformity: self-discipline; obedience

Security: stability of social order; health; sense of belonging

Not only do we find these values everywhere, we also find that, whether people live in urban North America or the African rainforest, whether in Shanghai or the Argentine pampas, people throughout the world agree about 98% of the time on the order of their importance.

Which is most important? Benevolence—doing unto others as you would have them do unto you.

Which is least important? Power.

In order of their importance, here's the whole list of values.

1. Benevolence
2. Self-direction
3. Universalism
4. Security
5. Conformity
6. Achievement
7. Hedonism
8. Stimulation
9. Tradition
10. Power

Values cannot distinguish one from another. In all essentials everyone agrees about what's good. Moreover, everyone agrees about how good something is compared with other good things. Actions that correspond with the Golden Rule are more important than safety or having fun, although they're all good things. Thus, people on both sides of the abortion debate agree on the value of life, even for unborn children, and the value on women's ability to make their own life choices. Both count as forms of Benevolence. They differ, just like political conservatives and liberals, on what counts as what. Some people count any fertilized ovum or fetus as an unborn child. Other people count only a fetus that may live outside the womb as an unborn child. Freedom comes from the active exercise of personal responsibility, for political conservatives. Freedom comes from authoritative regulation of inequalities for political liberals.

Cultural assumptions thus distinguish one culture from another and one individual from another. Differences in cultural assumptions produce differences in cultural norms. Cultural norms are the admonitions that tell us what we should do (or, should not do). If a fertilized ovum counts as a living being, you shouldn't kill it any more than you should kill your neighbor. To maximize freedom, you should minimize restrictions on personal choices imposed by authorities.

This Book and Our Story

Cultures, this book argues, consist of teams of people who, because they ground their understanding of the world on a common postulate about its nature, share a specific moral vision for a behavioral domain. Individuals cannot do things on their own. Cultures do things only when team behavior corresponds to that vision (more or less). Cultural effectiveness depends on the degree of correspondence. Cultures-as-teams succeeded and grew increasingly successful by selecting for a mind that produces new things and a series of cognitive biases that produce the clarity necessary for making a behavioral choice, emotionally load experiences to direct our attention to achievements and mistakes, and by requiring us to give great weight to cultural authority, forcing compliance with a specific moral vision. But cultures can kill us. We're here only because our mind also evolved another bias that, in the presence of evolutionarily significant threats, tells us to change assumptions and act according to another moral vision.

The short version of Our Story—with some specifics—goes something like this: intelligent information processing produces new ideas (h/t Homer Barnett and William Calvin) that our Interpreter (h/t Michael Gazzaniga) uses to speculate about the nature of the world and to reason about what those postulates imply about moral (aka "fair") behavior. Evolved cognitive biases (h/t more-people-than-we-can-shake-a-stick-at) quicken our ability to make choices based on experience with opportunities and dangers and to weight most heavily the consensus of ideas and behavioral responses of the people who constitute our community. The cognitive bias that weights the risk of choice alternatives (h/t Amos Tversky and Daniel Kahneman) in ways that force us to hate losing more than we love winning produces sharp behavioral differences. Treatment judged fair elicits commitment to that community and the coordinated (teamwork) behavior that allows us to achieve orders of reality that individuals cannot. Treatment judged unfair elicits defensive action that changes cultures.

Part I of this book describes how intelligence produces imaginary things that imply a moral order for specific behavioral domains. Chapter 1 describes and illustrates how intelligence produces imaginary things that embody a moral vision. Chapter 2 illustrates with the imaginary postulates that apply to a health culture, two business cultures (food sales and sex sales), a political culture, the college party culture, and cultures resting on postulates about the nature of people that tell us how we should interact with other people across behavioral domains like health, business, politics, and partying. Chapter 3 shows what happens when behavior corresponds with the specific moral visions described in Chapter 2. Chapter 4 shows how foragers—our ancestors—used multiple morally ordered behaviors to flourish and populate the globe.

Part II explains how evolved biases force compliance with the moral orders that correspond to specific cultures and why the resulting codependencies selected so strongly for the biases that produced this effect. Chapter 5 identifies the means by which our minds imbue cultures with coercive force. Chapter 6 points out that the agency of cultures may kill you, if you let it. Chapter 7 describes how and under what circumstances evolved-choice frames give agency to individuals to try new ways when old ways yield dangerous effects.

Humans thus evolved to respond to each other in ways that form teams. We cannot act independently of teams and the moral vision they enact, and they direct the course of our lives even when we remain blissfully unaware of their power or direction. We call these things cultures. Which explains why we're wrong when we imagine that individuals—humans, organizations, or nations—count as the primary agents. Poverty can't be due to poor decisions by the poor any more than campus rapes occur because of predatory men and will go away once you indoctrinate college freshmen to treat each other well. Bullies cannot make their targets commit suicide any more than poverty can breed sociopaths, drug use, or crime. The concluding "lessons learned" chapter explores some of the implications of Our Story for understanding such issues as poverty, social justice, bullying, rape, the dangers of cultural incompetence and why *Question Authority* shouldn't be treated as a mere slogan. We focus on lessons for cultural change—particularly how and why we may switch from the cultures we followed since childhood to a more satisfying and useful set.

Part I

On Cultures

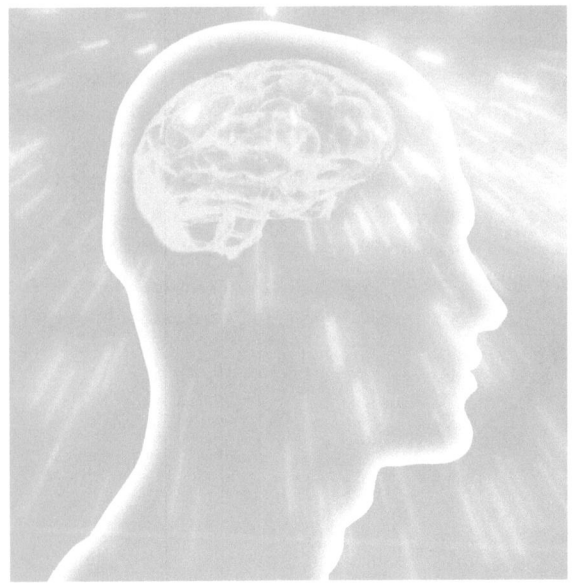

Chapter 1

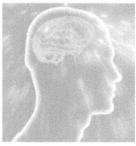

Cultures Originate in Intelligent Minds

We create and maintain codependencies that enable our survival and open the possibility that we might thrive. Our minds do this in the normal course of their operation, as Clifford Geertz pointed out 60 years ago. We call these outcomes *cultures*. We've used other labels at various times and places— institutions, world views, visions of the world, schemas, models, and public opinion, to name a few. Each culture consists of one or more shared postulates or assumptions about the things that make up our world. Labels distinguish one thing from another. The postulates that ground a culture yield shared corollary understandings—rules, expectations—about what we should and should not do, which we call *cultural norms*. This moral universe guides our interpretation of and response to environmental variation. The most important form of environmental variation consists of what the people with whom we live say and do—and don't say or do.

This chapter describes how *intelligence*, one component of the organ system we call the *central nervous system*, creates ever-changing postulates about the nature of the world in which we live and moral corollaries that tell us how we should or should not live in it.

"You" Comes from Your Mind

Living things must identify and respond to the properties of their environments or soon they won't be alive. Whether the organism is a bacterium, a plant, a fish, or a person, for instance, it must be able to "know" food and danger when it finds them, and it must "know" what to do when it encounters either. Genes construct mechanisms that permit living things to keep track of changes in the world in which they live. We call these things *senses*. Environments make themselves known to organisms, and organisms track changes in those environments through sound, odor, taste, form, light-spectrum absorption, and other forms of sensation. Senses identify the physical properties of material stimuli and, among some organisms, relay that information along cell pathways to a coordinating center, the central nervous system.

Central nervous systems consist of billions of cells called *neurons*, and, for each of these, another nine glial cells that support neuronal functions. Neurons consist of dendrites that receive information from the axons of other neurons across a synapse. Information passes through neurons as electrical impulses. An insulating fatty layer of glial cells called a *myelin sheath* speeds ion-channel- powered information flow. Information passes from one neuron to another across a gap called a *synapse* in the form of a chemical (a neurotransmitter, or modulator) released from an axon and taken up by a dendrite.

Neurons thus provide our means of information reception, transmission, storage, and assembly. You—your self, who you are and what you do—emerge as the outcome of these processes. If something alters how these processes work, who you are and what you do also changes.

Some simple examples:

- How much and how fast your neurons release a neurotransmitter we call Substance P determines, among many things, if and the extent to which you feel pain.
- You may have noticed feeling wonderful after vigorous physical activity or listening to "thrilling music" and (if you're a woman) that sex makes your headache go away. These effects come from the release of neurotransmitters, enkephalins, and endorphins.
- If you suffer multiple sclerosis, it's because damaged myelin sheaths dramatically reduce intraneuronal information flow.
- Alcohol consumption inhibits the flow of sodium ions that power intraneuronal information flows and thus makes actions that depend on reaction time dangerous.
- Your mother's testosterone/estradiol balance during pregnancy created your balance of feminine and masculine characteristics.
- Amphetamines produce a nice high, which collapses into depression. The high comes from an increased release of norepinephrine and dopamine. The depression comes from overproduction of these hormones, which interferes with resynthesis of another hormone, serotonin.
- Men's minds release of the hormone oxytocin tells women other than their girlfriend or wife that these men aren't interested in a relationship.
- Without the gene to produce FOXP2 proteins, you, along with other mammals and birds, cannot communicate effectively—whether you communicate

with language, songs, echolocation signals, or ultrasonic screams. The relative quantity of these proteins in a human brain's language control area explains why women generally talk much more than men.

Brain functions produce far more dramatic changes in who you are and what you do. For example, emotional weighting of memories and framing choices as gains or losses fundamentally shapes our actions and is regulated by the limbic system. One limbic system component, the hypothalamus, controls the endocrine system via a series of hormones. Variations in one hormone, dopamine, tend to correspond with the enjoyment, pleasure, and excitement with which a person experiences new stimuli. Variation in a second, norepinephrine, tends to correspond with perceived clarity and confidence in a person's interpretation of experience. Variation in a third, serotonin, tends to correspond with the speed with which a person responds to danger. Robert Cloninger created a model of alcoholism from variation in these hormones, but you don't have to drink to see how variation in the level of these hormones produce dramatically different people.

For example:

- If levels of dopamine, norepinephrine, and serotonin are all low, the *you* produced doesn't like change (stubborn, risk-averse) and finds the world dangerous, because its mind produces both ambiguous interpretations of the environment and responds to danger slowly. Defensive action vacillates between little or none to panicky and unexpected mood swings and flashes of violence. If we raise serotonin levels, we find a stubborn, risk-averse person who finds the world dangerous but who may respond reasonably to threats, without radical vacillation. Both hormone mixes produce narcissists, who view the world as it relates solely to themselves. Uniformly low hormone levels, however, produce "angry narcissists"—the names Alex Baldwin and Barack Obama come to mind. A shift to high levels of serotonin, by contrast, produce "moral narcissists" —George W. Bush and Judith Butler come to mind—who rationalize their view with a religious ideology. This set of hormone levels may generally characterize "whistle-blowers."

- A mind with low levels of norepinephrine and serotonin but high levels of dopamine, who takes suicidal risks because he or she doesn't recognize or respond quickly to survival threats, would be a prime candidate for Wendy Northcutt's *The Darwin Awards* (2000). Like Rashaad, 19, who played Russian roulette with a .45 caliber semiautomatic pistol—but only once, since he forgot to remove the cartridge in the chamber. Or, the Arizona man who chose a thunderstorm as a time to urinate through the bars of a wrought-iron safety fence. Lightning struck the fence and traveled to the ground but also up the urine stream to explode his penis.

- A mind with high levels of all three hormones, who finds enjoyment in novelty, makes confident evaluations of experience and responds quickly and confidently to danger, produces a self we characterize as a heroic adventurer and leader, someone who changes the world. Like Moses, Harriet Tubman, Winston Churchill, George Washington, Geronimo, Golda Meir, Abraham Lincoln, Simon Bolivar, Davy Crockett, Martin Luther King Jr., Chief Joseph, and Frederick Douglass.

Our Minds Create New Things

In his 1932 book Remembering, F. C. Bartlett made the observation that each of us constructs our understanding of the world by combining things we perceive with things we remember. In his 1953 book Innovation, Homer Barnett added the observation that this constructive process necessarily created new things, qualitatively different from other things, and he exhaustively reviewed the ways in which new things came into being. Barnett argued that we construct new things by a simple process. If by assumption we make one thing (or a part of one thing) the same as another thing (or one or more of its parts), each counts as the same thing, and one may substitute for the other. The result is something qualitatively different from the old things from which they are made. New things thus come into being when we substitute one thing for another.

Albert Einstein, for example, knew from Galileo via Newton that a fixed frame for evaluating the movement of one object relative to another did not exist and that the laws of physics applied to all frames of reference. Traveling home after many hours of discussing a conflict between Newtonian and Maxwellian physics with his friend Michele Besso, Einstein imagined that if you looked at a clock while moving away from it at the speed of light the clock would appear to be stopped, while the clock in your hand would indicate the passage of time normally. This phenomenon meant that it was impossible to define time independent of a frame of reference and that what counts as a unit of time depended on velocity. He thus recognized that objects that move at the same speed as each other (an inertial frame) counted as one among many frames of reference. He substituted this specific kind of frame for the set of all frames and concluded that the laws of physics are the same in all inertial frames. He knew from Maxwell that the speed of light, c, was a constant. If the speed of light is a constant, it must count as a law of physics, so the speed of light must be a constant in all inertial frames. He thus created his two principles of Special Relativity. The world hasn't been the same since.

Player pianos came into being after someone equated holes in a paper roll with fingers that could strike a piano key and recognized that a specific pattern of holes would code for the specific pattern of key strokes that produced a musical score. Edwin Votey made the first useful player piano in 1895. But the idea of coded holes in paper goes back to 1725 and provided the basis for constructing a loom for weaving intricate patterns. Herman Hollerith borrowed this idea from his brother-in-law, who was in the silk-weaving business and who had told him about the looms for Jacquard weaving, to produce cards with which to process the 1890 U.S. census. Hollerith cards were, in retrospect, a critical step in the development of information technologies. The idea of things that coded for other things later provided the prototype for supposing that genetic material comprised codes for the construction of proteins.

As Barnett pointed out, we substituted horses for people to turn millstones, presses, waterlifts, and treadmills. Later, we substituted engines for horses in these and other activities to create the material basis of the Industrial Revolution. Active development of engines followed from Torricelli's announcement in 1643 that air exerts pressure at sea level. Soon afterward, people tried to use this pressure to do things by creating a vacuum into which air would force a piston. In 1654, van Guericke constructed a pump that drew air instead of water from a closed container. In 1680, Huygens substituted gunpowder for a pump. Huygen's assistant, Denis Papin, substituted steam for gunpowder when he reasoned that water vapor had a force, like air. Papin constructed an engine and, in the presence of the members of the Royal Society of London, demonstrated its ability to raise a counterweight. In the early 1700s, Thomas Newcomen constructed a heavy-duty replica of Papin's laboratory exhibit that pumped water from mines instead of raising blocks and replaced horses on treadmills. In 1769, James Watt placed the condenser in its own chamber to transform Newcomen's design into a much more efficient and useful steam engine. Huygens's experiments with gunpowder as a source of controlled force also took another direction. In the 1780s, Alessandro Volta showed that an electrical spark could explode air (mixed with hydrogen), and, in 1799, LeBon built a machine powered by exploding coal gas. In 1859, Lenoir substituted benzene for gas, substituted his piston and combustion chamber for the comparable elements of a steam engine, and mounted his engine on a carriage or a wagon as a substitute for horse or steam power. He thus produced the first useful vehicle driven by an internal combustion engine.

Goatsie

In the mid-1980s, I lived in a small redwood grove overrun with brambles outside Trinidad, California. A friend who lived in nearby Eureka kept a goat who loved brambles. So it came to be that for a few years Goatsie lived with my family from fall through spring to fatten on brambles and return well-fed to his city home.

One fall day, I staked Goatsie just outside my house so he could trim back a barberry bush that intruded into the driveway and checked on him periodically through the window. The second time I checked, Goatsie raised his left hind hoof to scratch his side. Shortly after, Goatsie looked around at the ground, which made no sense since the ground held no food. Turned out that Goatsie wasn't looking for food. He found a stick, moved it around his mouth, turned around and tried to scratch his side. That stick was too short. Goatsie dropped it and searched for a longer stick. As with the first, Goatsie settled the stick in his mouth and twisted around to scratch. Because this second stick was long enough, Goatsie could scratch, but because it was straight he couldn't exert force effectively.

Goatsie dropped that stick, looked around, picked up another long one with several forks, bit off extraneous branches, and twisted slightly and scratched away in ecstasy for nearly a minute. I stood there dumbfounded. Goatsie had equated a stick with his hoof and thus had imagined, constructed, and used a tool.

Evolutionary Origins of Innovation-Induced Uncertainty

Minds can't evolve ways of working like these unless they increase a being's ability to survive and reproduce. Think of "Life" as an open-energy system regulated by nucleic acids. By definition, all forms of life require regular inputs of energy and nutrients—resources, in short. Selection must favor any property that improves or optimizes resource access, will concentrate innovations that do so, and will build relatively advantageous means of acquiring resources and will eliminate innovations and interfere with the process of resource acquisition. Selection favors innovation-induced uncertainty only when a mind that produces random novelty—irrespective of uncertainty—improves resource reliability. Random novelty improves resource reliability only when resource location and timing changes unpredictably in far less time than a living organism's generation length. Selection will favor organisms that change both their behavior and their concepts in ways that optimize or improve their access to resources. Hence, selection favors organisms that generate conceptual and behavioral innovations in the presence of resource changes. Since resource changes cannot be predicted, selection must favor organisms that generate conceptual and behavioral innovations continually. Selection also favors organisms that match conceptual innovations with corresponding behavioral innovations, whichever occurs first.

It does not follow that the innovations that emerge will optimize or improve resource access in a new structure of resources. Similarly, it does not follow that individuals will correctly identify and choose to utilize those innovations that optimize or improve resource access. On the contrary, resource access is optimized or improved by behavioral and conceptual response diversity. Behavioral and conceptual response diversity is constrained if organisms can change their behavior only by reference to genetically identified experiential cues. It follows, somewhat paradoxically, that selection favors (1) individuals who cannot invariably generate innovations that optimize resource access and (2) individuals who cannot invariably identify and correctly choose the innovations that optimize resource access.

However, it does follow that selection favors those innovations and those decisions that do optimize or improve resource access. It also follows that selection favors those individuals who can rectify their mistakes most rapidly. Hence, selection concentrates conceptual and behavioral innovations that improve or optimize resource access. In short, selection favors organisms that have genes that control (indeed, that would dictate) the process of concept formation but that do not control the conceptual outcome of this process.

We're not alone in our ability to create new things and turn them into something useful. We now understand that we share many of these features of mind with creatures as diverse as birds and rodents and octopi, so the evolutionary history of this mechanism must be very, very old. In Tel Aviv, for example, crows fish with bait. Woodpecker finches in the Galapagos Islands make and use tools. Cormorants in Japan count. New Caledonia crows modify existing tools to make them better. Harry Jerison's 1973 *Evolution of the Brain and Intelligence* suggests that a mind that processed information in creative ways may have first appeared 50 million years ago and perhaps as early as 200 million years ago.

New Things Come from Thinking a Thought

In 1996, William Calvin suggested a means by which the brain continually manufactures new things. In the late 1940s, the psychologist Donald Hebb observed that associative memory seemed to stem from groups of neurons that work together when processing sensory input. Our neocortex, the sheath of neurons most recently added in the brain's evolution, consists largely of pyramidal neurons that run through a number of strata. The bottom two strata contain pyramidal neurons that send axons to the thalamus. The one immediately above these receives inputs from the thalamus. The top strata contain neurons with axons that branch sideways up to 10,000 times, which terminate at varying distances.

The synapses of these cells tend to be characterized by distinctive circuit properties. One consists of a propensity to retain traces of earlier activity, which quickens reactivation. The other consists of the common presence of postsynaptic receptors that strengthen the signal of inputs that arrive in clusters. Because they do not leave these strata, they thus appear to process information solely within the neocortex.

Calvin argues that the distinctive features of our neocortex provide the means for effective Hebbian cell assembly activity. Any one Hebbian cell assembly consists, minimally, of 100 minicolumns containing around 10,000 pyramidal neurons organized in a hexagonal pattern. But cell assemblies do not consist of discrete sets of cells. Rather, they appear as mosaics of electrical activity that dynamically form and re-form across the billions and billions of neurons that make up the human neocortex. They thus create distinctive firing patterns with both spatial and temporal dimensions.

The memories you accumulate from the sensory fields of your past and present consist of bits and pieces of information. Your mind doesn't remember coherent thoughts or actions. Your mind absorbs and stores things such as variations in color, intensity of light, physical size and shape, odor, taste, feel, and sound as well as relationships between things, the properties of things, and events and sequences of events. Your mind constructs coherent thoughts and actions by assigning relationships to and among the bits and pieces of information of your mind. Some memories may reside in specific cells. The vast majority, more likely, consist of firing patterns that code for a piece of sensory information. To dunk a basketball or think of God, the things of our mind must undergo an assembly process of the kind Donald Hebb imagined, the output of which Bartlett and Barnett described.

At any moment in time, huge numbers of cell assemblies may be active. Their activities may mutually excite each other, capture the information processes of other assemblies, and produce firing synchrony. The cell assembly, Calvin argues, may record the features of a thing, and its firing patterns may code for the thing and constitute the neural analog of an idea. The entrainment process that generates synchrony determines the construction outcome—which specific memory traces get linked with which other specific memories.

I called these processes *intelligence*. Intelligent beings think in ways that invariably lead to new and unexpected ways of looking at the world. They thus generate an unusual degree of behavioral flexibility. All living things, plants as well as people, must process information from sensory fields. That processing may or may not involve information storage or the integration of stored information with information recently received. But to say that an intelligent mind creates ideas does not mean that genes cease to influence behavior in important ways. Ideas are coded bundles of information that are more than the sum of their parts, because they integrate information from a variety of senses, including information about the relationship among ideas.

Specific behaviors or complex sets of coordinated activities and movements embody those codes. Thus, ideas and behaviors cannot be created unless genes construct neural circuitry that allows different kinds of information from one sense to be related to different kinds of information from several or from all senses, including relationships among different forms of information. Moreover, genes dictate that experience will be stored in a particular form as one or another or several kinds of memory and that we will construct ideas and behavior by a process that integrates information from a variety of sources within specific constraints of time and complexity. Genes thus control the processes by which intelligent minds work. They just don't dictate the outcome. Intelligent forms of life thus have a built-in mechanism that continuously generates random conceptual innovation and behavioral change.

Random (maybe chaotic) processes intrude on the constructive process of information transmission within and between cell assemblies, however. Neural processing is ephemeral and may become blocked by weak synaptic links; traces may linger that may facilitate the re-creation of a specific firing pattern, or of any part of one; and different cell assemblies may overlap or otherwise intrude on one another. In the process, they may drop features, add them, or substitute one thing for another. Our brains thus invariably and necessarily produce the variation we see in our ideas and behavior. No two experiences come to us the same way, and no experience of the same thing duplicates earlier ones—which means that each of us cannot help but see the world differently at different times and places, act in ways that may surprise us, and make mistakes. The manner in which our brains produce ideas necessarily involve substitutions of the kind that produce new things.

But It Makes for Mistake-Prone Minds

The things of our world of experience thus consist of speculations. We may take for granted that a material world exists independently of our imagining. But that world doesn't tell us what's there. We have to guess at its parts and how they fit together, or how they don't. All human knowledge thus rests on assumptions.

Intelligent beings' imagination produces a continuous flow of new ideas and behaviors. But specific novelties originate unexpectedly and invariably contain imperfections. Assumptions, of course, are true by definition. They can't be proved. All assumptions probably contain errors, some are plainly wrong, but some assumptions prove useful. We label important ones, and, however ambiguously in specific cases, we differentiate one from another by defining each by a set of properties. A door is a door, not a chair, a house, or a person, although there are many kinds of doors. A chair is a thing you can sit on—it has a more-or-less flat surface about 18″ by 18″ square placed at varying distances (ordinarily at least 6″ and no more than 24″) above the ground by stabilizing supports we call legs and an attached vertical surface we call a back. We call the same thing with a round surface a stool. We call the same thing without a back and with a larger surface a table.

Many people know what doors are. Many fewer realize that a woman can marry a ghost and bear his children, or that a married woman with children can marry another woman and father still more children as the husband of the new wife. Yet, ghost marriages occurred among groups as dissimilar as Nuer pastoralists in the southern Sudan and Chinese migrants to Singapore. Female husbands occurred among the Fon of Dahomey and more than 30 other African societies, including the Nuer.

A more telling way to think about anthropological curiosities like these: the meaning of a thing (anything, everything) depends on your assumptions.

Answers to the questions "Do you roast your dog or take it for a walk; snack on ants or poison them?" depend, for example, on what counts as food, pets, and pests. Imagine a father, a daughter, and a grandson. Do the three people belong to the same family? The answer is no if they assume that family relationships flow only through females (a matrilineal system of reckoning kin) and yes, otherwise. If the father is "black," is the grandson "black"? By what criteria?

Photo on the next page shows the remains of one of three girls beheaded as they returned home from school in Indonesia. Fierce satisfaction will fill your mind if you count what you see as infidels who received their due because they were Christians. What fills your mind? Whatever, it depends on the assumptions you use to make sense of the information in the photographs.

The speculative postulates that our mind imagines provide the foundations of cultures and come out of our consciousness in the form a story told by our mind's Interpreter. Consciousness and our Interpreter plausibly evolved as an uncertainty-reduction regulator. Our Interpreter spins stories that can't be proved true or false and that thus (and

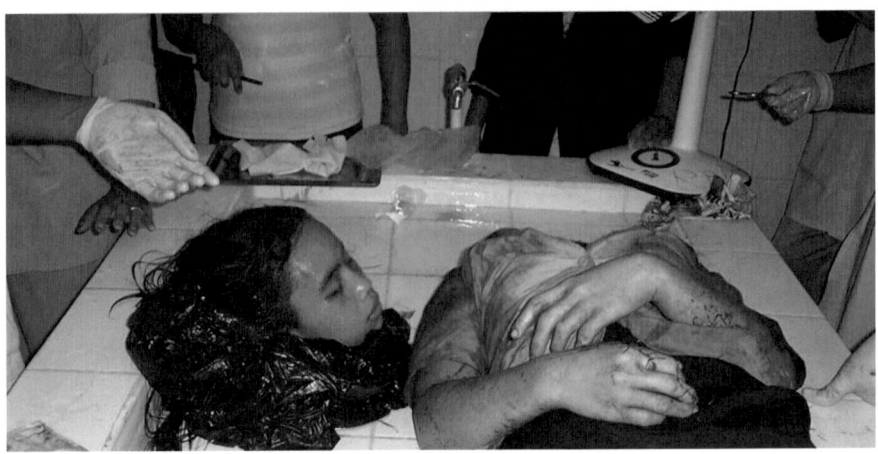

despite speeding our ability to rectify mistakes) induce uncertainty. The stories reduce this uncertainty by quickly moving the products of short-term memory into long-term memory in the form of rules that tell us what we and others should do—how, for example, we should respond to norm violations. Postulates thus rationalize corollaries that define a moral universe. As mentioned earlier, academics call these corollaries *cultural norms,* or *expectations.* Our minds evaluate the correspondence between specific sensory experiences and our standards about how the world of experience should be. We thus use this correspondence to detect and respond to norm violations. If we imagine that people are naturally good but, being human, make mistakes, we should respond by pointing out a mistake and helping the person know how to not repeat that mistake. If we imagine that people will exploit you if they can and treat you well only if they must, we should respond by protecting ourselves.

Morality as Evolutionary By-Product of Intelligence

Every culture rests on a specific set of speculations, each set of which thus creates a moral order for a specific behavioral domain. Morality, a sense of right and wrong, therefore emerged as a simple consequence of the evolutionary advantages that accrue to a mind that creates imaginative worlds.

Our evolved central nervous system presents us with a central dilemma: why should we assume that a particular way of thinking about the world of experience is not merely a figment of one's imagination—that a label defined in a particular way, that means used to distinguish one phenomenon from another (that is, measurement), and that claimed relationships between one phenomenon and any other(s) correspond with the world of experience in some meaningful way? Donald Campbell pointed out 40 years ago that research should thus consist of a search for ways to distinguish mental constructions that consist largely of fantasy from constructions that consist of less. Data collection should entail an active search for the errors that must pervade the constructs you use to formulate questions and make observations, the observations you make, and for the errors or bias attached to the times and places and people from whom you collected those data. This unending search for errors means that *iterative* data collection distinguishes good research from bad. Responsible investigators thus design each observation and question to test at least one part of a growing theoretical understanding. Note errors, ask for clarification, rethink the theory, and link microlevel observations and interviews with historical records and macrolevel trends that only time-series data can reveal. Then, do it all again. In short, the right thing to do, if we recognize our propensity for errors, is to find them and correct them.

We find moral orders whenever we find beings like Goatsie, who display creative imaginations. Imaginative postulates that apply to other living beings tell us how we should treat them. Long before discernibly human ancestors walked the earth, intelligent living things recognized that what goes around comes around. As Marc Bekoff and Jessica Pierce observe in their book *Wild Justice:*

> A teenage female elephant nursing an injured leg is knocked over by a rambunctious, hormone-laden teenage male. An older female sees this happen, chases the male away, and goes back to the younger female and touches her sore leg with her trunk. Eleven elephants rescue a group of captive antelope in KwaZulu-Natal; the matriarch undoes all of the latches on the gates of the enclosure with her trunk and lets the gate swing open so the antelope can escape. A rat in a cage refuses to push a lever for food when it sees that another rat receives an electric shock as a result. A male Diana monkey who has learned to insert a token into a slot to obtain food helps a female who can't get the hang of the trick, inserting the token for her and allowing her to eat the food reward. A female fruit-eating bat helps an unrelated female give birth by showing her how to hang in the proper way. A cat named Libby leads her elderly, deaf, and blind dog friend, Cashew, away from obstacles and to food. In a group of chimpanzees at the Arnhem Zoo in The Netherlands individuals punish other chimpanzees who are late for dinner because no one eats until everyone's present. A large male dog wants to play with a younger and more submissive male. The big male invites his younger partner to play and restrains himself, and biting his younger companion gently and allowing him to bite gently in return. (2009: 152–53)

That recognition, in turn, gave evolutionary advantages to a set of cognitive mechanisms that brought clarity to ambiguity, distinguished what worked from what doesn't, and produced increasingly effective cooperative teams.

Chapter 2

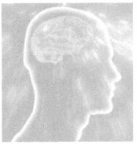

Cultures Establish Moral Orders

In *The Law of Primitive Man* (1954), E. A. Hoebel showed in detail how easily we could describe cultures by a set of postulates about the nature of our world, each of which implied a set of corollaries that established moral orders for specific behavioral domains. His chapter on the Eskimo, for example, started with the observation that people in the Arctic took for granted that animals possess an emotional intelligence, as humans do, constitute active components of human worlds, and dominate humans in some life domains. Most Americans probably have never seriously thought about animals beyond their appearance as a steak, chop, or rib on the dinner table or the enjoyment of pets or the interest that exotics elicit. Among foragers throughout the world, however, "animal" means something you have to find, kill, and butcher before you can eat it. Plus, if you don't carry out these activities consistently, you'll die.

If we postulate, as most Americans do, that animals count as food, we should eat meat. And most Americans do. Most Americans make exclusions, however. Pets do not count as food. You should not eat your pet. We assign names to pets, so we commonly apply the operational rule: you should not eat an animal you named (my horse Dude, my breeding male French Lop rabbit Thumper, or my bramble clearer Goatsie) or is commonly given names (Chewy the Jack Russell Terrier or Grindl the 20-pound cat). Note that this moral world excludes mention of the life conditions and means by which an animal becomes steaks, chops, or ribs on the table.

PETA (People for the Ethical Treatment of Animals) postulates that animals cannot count as food (and many other things). They advocate that you should not hunt, wear leather or fur, keep a pet, or eat meat. Their website elaborates and concludes: "only prejudice allows us to deny others the rights that we expect to have for ourselves.

Whether it's based on race, gender, sexual orientation, or species, prejudice is morally unacceptable. If you wouldn't eat a dog, why eat a pig? Dogs and pigs have the same capacity to feel pain, but it is prejudice based on species that allows us to think of one animal as a companion and the other as dinner."

The word *prejudice* impedes understanding by pointing to an irrelevancy. When someone feels repulsed by the thought of eating a dog but can't wait to feast on baby-back ribs, it's merely how that culture identifies what counts as food. PETA, and vegans more generally, count carrots, rice, and apples as food with no more empirical grounding than the bulk of the U.S. population count pigs as food and dogs as not-food. They claim, albeit without evidence, that some living things do not experience suffering. Plants exhibit "intelligent" forms of awareness, "know" when attacked, and respond by activating specific defense mechanisms — see Michael Pollan's nice summary "The Intelligent Plant," in *The New Yorker* (12/23/2013), or specific studies like those of Rex Cocroft and Heidi Apell at the University of Missouri (http://www.agweb.com/article/plants-can-hear-pests-attack/). On its website, PETA gives great weight to the following quote by PETA founder Ingrid Newkirk: "When it comes to pain, love, joy, loneliness, and fear, a rat is a pig is a dog is a boy. Each one values his or her life and fights the knife." So do carrots, rice, and apples.

We create a very different moral world of death and life, however, once we postulate that, before we kill it, what counts as food for us exhibits an emotional intelligence just like ours. Most contemporary hunters, whether their day job consists of hunting, auto mechanic, or day trader, understand that this means that we should acknowledge and show respect to a fellow being who gave its life to sustain ours. The moral order of respect given to the spirits who support our life takes many forms. A hunter may apologize for killing an animal or cry after the animal's death. Before a hunt, the hunter may pray to ask a deer, or bear, or moose, to give its life so the hunter and the hunter's family may live. While searching for food, a hunter should show respect by moving slowly and carefully and quietly. Hunters should allow animals to teach them about their spirits and their worlds and how they use resources to live. After a kill, a hunter should butcher the animal by established rituals and treat the carcass with the respect due another intelligent being. The successful hunter might return beaver bones to the water in which the beaver lived, or post a moose's beard on a tree, or hold a feast to celebrate a bear, or bury at the death site the casing of the cartridge used to kill an elk.

Cultures Define Activity Domains

All this reminds us that the things of our world come from our imagination and possess no intrinsic meaning. The meaning of a thing comes from the postulates our minds create to understand our sensory world of experience. Labels and their definitions (implied or explicit) tell us the domain's inventory. Postulates about the nature of the domain tell us how we should act.

An American Oral Health Culture

For example, the things that constitute the American culture of oral health include different kinds of teeth (good teeth and bad teeth), jaws, gums, blood, pain, pain killers (aspirin, generic and trademarked forms of ibuprofen, lidocaine), cavities, fillings, toothpaste, toothbrushes, dental floss, dental instruments, dental visits, dentists, dental hygienists, dental offices and staff, dental appointments, antibiotic mouthwash, waiting times, anxiety, fear, terror, insurance, diets, nutrients, responsibility, transportation, costs (in time, money), and dental procedures (like cleaning, root canals, crowns, bridges, and extraction). The culture rests on the postulate that oral health problems do not kill, and many go away on their own or respond well to self-treatment—keep your teeth clean and eat in ways that promote oral health, and you'll never have an oral health problem. Moreover, if you run into a tooth problem, it progresses so slowly that it rarely requires immediate attention, and an eventual dental visit (maybe several follow-up visits) eliminates the problem. Symptoms of oral health problems include sensitive teeth, tooth pain, receding gums, bleeding gums, and cavities. If you want to avoid or correct an oral health problem, you should brush your teeth twice daily, floss, use an antibiotic mouthwash, and visit a dentist twice a year. You should also consider supplementing these activities by modifying your diet to make it low in sugar, high in calcium, and rich in vitamins and minerals. Because teeth problems are easy to spot and easy to prevent, moreover, the culture holds that oral health problems reflect an individual failure to take care of one's teeth. Bad teeth mean that you did not do what you should have to maintain good teeth.

Business Cultures—Selling Food, Selling Sex

The things that make up a business culture vary dramatically with the thing sold. For example, in Liberia, farmers sell food to consumers and bulkers. The latter move large quantities of food from rural areas to urban areas, where they sell to retailers, who sell to consumers. The Liberian culture of food distribution thus consists of things like rice, palm oil, eddos, cassava, fish, meat, crawfish, collard greens, potato greens, chicken soup, and other dietary items, a variety of kinds of selling locations (periodic markets, payday markets, daily markets), market stalls, and a variety of kinds of transport operators, farmers, bulkers, and retailers, primarily differentiated by their status as "good customer," fellow retailer, or kin—and risks. As of the late 20th century, Liberia's capital city, Monrovia, had nine major marketplaces and two incipient markets that offered every variety of domestic produce, craft items, and perhaps 200 varieties of imports, including foodstuffs, cloth, clothing, jewelry, and sundries. Boys and girls hawked popcorn, biscuits, water, eggs, and frozen cubes of soft drink along the streets, at bus and taxi depots, in residential areas, on the outskirts, and occasionally within marketplaces. House sellers were with few exceptions (for instance, neighbors who, for companion-

Chapter 2   Cultures Establish Moral Orders   37

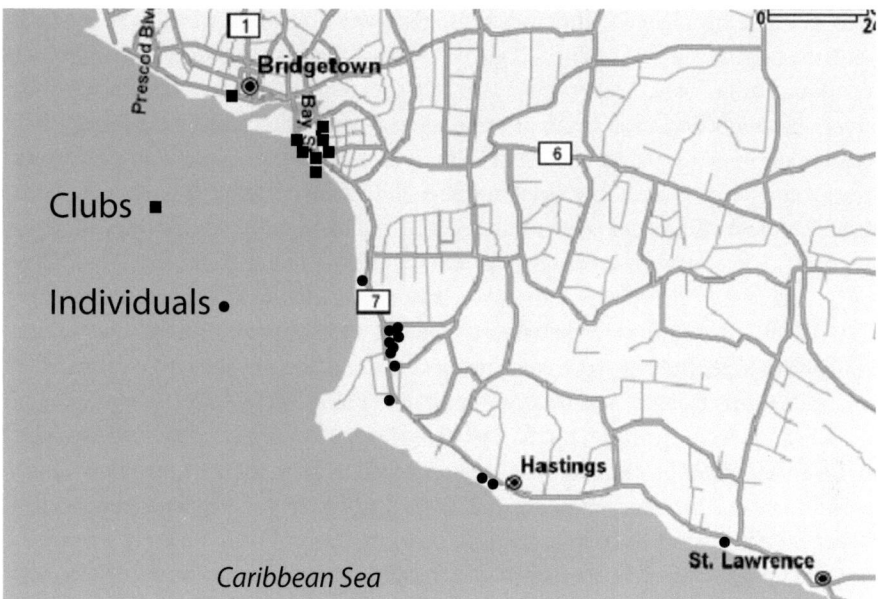

Figure 2.1

ship, chose to sit with one another) spatially dispersed single traders vending from their doorsteps. These firms, each stocking from five to seven items, catered to a restricted, generalized demand for staple foodstuffs: peppers, palm oil, rice, bouillon cubes, dried fish and meat, and occasionally candies, gum, kola, oranges, roasted corn, and plantain. Along the major walkways, at road intersections, schools, hospitals, shops, stores, and supermarkets, were petty traders. Each of these stocked two or three items and catered to a demand from a larger, more dispersed population for snack items (candies, biscuits, gum, matches, cigarettes, kola, peanuts); or, depending on the season, oranges or roasted corn or plantain; or, at the supermarkets, a wide variety of fresh fruit.

The Bajan culture of commercial sex—known in Barbados as "de fas life"—consists of clients (visitors and locals), service providers (ladies of the evening; "ladies" for short, also known as "prostitutes," "whores," and "fares"), semicompetitors (part-time call girls and miscellaneous part-timers, some of whom solicit at mid- or upper-scale clubs, plus some females aged 10–18 who occasionally skip school to sell sex, women who function as mistresses or courtesans, set up in apartments by the wealthy, and Deebee-deebee girls and beachboys), selling locations (the street, the club), sexual services ("respectable" and "kinky"), and police. "De fas life" exhibits two major configurations, The Street and The Club, despite individual variability from site to site and person to person (see Figure 2.1).

Beginning around 10 P.M., or earlier on the weekends, women (mostly in their 20s and early 30s) walk out of "de Hole" onto the road in twos and threes and stroll on The

Street in the balmy night air. Thus they begin their working hours, which may last until 5 or 6 the next morning if business is good. Ladies at their posts issue a distinctive and attention-getting "sssst," beckon their prospect(s) closer, and ask him if he is lonely or wants a blow-job. Some women wear ordinary working clothes, mostly old dresses, but occasionally only a tee-shirt and tights. However, most women wear shiny, revealing dresses, fancy hairstyles, heavy facial makeup, and lots of perfume. Occasionally, both Barbadians and visitors discover they hired a man instead of the woman they thought they hired. Transvestite men occasionally work with the women. Some, like "Paul," cannot be confused with women. Others are regularly confused with women. Men like "David," who worked the area between the Hilton and the Island Inn until (as rumor has it) he died recently of AIDS, reportedly could consistently perform oral sex on a man or be the recipient of anal intercourse without being discovered.

The Club, by contrast, lies not far east of the bridge that gives Bridgetown its name, on the upper end of Bay St. and on an adjacent road, Nelson St. The Club takes up the second story in a two-story building, but its public domain encompasses an area only 20 feet wide by 30 feet long. Its entrance is dark, and the stairway walls are grungy. A bar takes up one corner. The owner-manager stands behind the bar, serves drinks, and carefully watches the action. The action begins in the late morning, when cruise ships are in port, and ends around 4 or 5 the next morning. At 11 in the morning, things are quiet, except for the jukebox, whose blaring never stops. A small group of men talk and drink together. A few men sit alone quietly drinking beer, rum, or gin. Two women sit at each of two tables, talking and laughing and sipping beer. Another woman works behind and around the bar. Another woman or two move between the tables, bar, and through a door that leads from the public domain to the toilets and the rooms where women live and conduct part of their work.

The women, in their late teens to early 30s, dress to advertise sexual services. None go nude. But none wears a bra, either. Very short skirts or Spandex tights, preferably a lace see-through version, are popular, as are loose or open shirts or tight elastic around the breasts. Women with skirts hike them up high on their thighs when they sit. Women in tights sit with legs spread wide. Occasionally, a woman in lace Spandex moves with the music, stands up to move her hips more freely, slowly and rhythmically touching her breasts, buttocks, and crotch. During the day, most clients are visitors. During the evening, most are Barbadian. Visitors who come to The Club during the day mainly comprise the crew and, to some extent, the passengers of cruise ships. Visitors who come to The Club in the evening come from the on-island tourist population. The Club's management posts cruise ship schedules so the ladies can plan ahead. Cruise ships dock regularly throughout the year. The winter tourist season sees the largest number of ships stop at the island, but specific ships come through every week or so.

The ladies come to know and look forward to seeing regular clients from the ships. Conversely, the crew come to have their own favorite ladies, whom they visit regularly when in port. Newcomers, whether crew or passengers, usually find The Club by being taken there by friends or directed there by an acquaintance. Sometimes ladies meet the ships at the port and direct business to The Club. By 2 in the afternoon, all the women working at The Club will have appeared and worked the room. Sales start slowly. But by mid-afternoon perhaps half a dozen ladies will have made sales. Ladies and their clients slip quietly into the back for periods of 5 to 30 minutes. Occasionally, men leave. Arrivals more than replace those who do. Sales pick up during the afternoon and slacken around 4, when crew and passengers return to their ship. Business turns up again in the early evening and continues until dawn the next day.

In both Liberia and Barbados, however, the central actors in the business culture consist of one-person firms run by single, managing entrepreneurs whose central aim is to acquire money with which to feed, clothe, and house themselves and their families. Profits come from sales, so to feed, clothe, and house themselves, sellers should create a reliable client base and enlarge it when and if possible. Collusion provides the ideal way to do this. Collusion allows a trader to purchase only the best food a farmer produces at low prices and travel to and from urban markets cheaply and quickly, and it allows retailers to sell food at prices that guarantee good profits even when their food spoils.

Fortunately or unfortunately, according to your point of view, few barriers to trade mean many competitors. In the real world of food and sex sales, entrepreneurs work from a common postulate—"We are all on our own." The best strategy? The one Zig Ziglar stated memorably—"You will get all you want in life if you help enough other people get what they want." How do you help enough other people get what they want?

Whether you sell food or sex, undercut or match the lowest competitive price. Do better by offering valuable personal services, over and above cash prices. If you sell food, offer the best of your current produce, a "dash" of additional produce, credit, and perhaps an occasional loan—and in any case credit or loans on easy terms. Such customers may be allowed purchases when they do not have the correct amount, and, although exceptional, a few retailers deliver goods to their "customers'" houses and pay the transportation costs for "customers" who have to travel a considerable distance to market. When given a choice between the same-quality items, as often as not people report that it is better to purchase from a friend than to purchase for a lower price; in the long run, "the friend will help you." If the seller will not grant you credit, she will "consider" you and allow you to purchase for a lower than normal price when you are genuinely in need. As one man noted: "Some people buy from traders or relatives because the traders consider you the customer if you are a friend to that person. For instance, I went to the market. My intention was to get all of what I wanted. But because I was short a few cents, if there was a friend who is selling this particular article, he will surely consider me and give me that article for $.05 if the last price is $0.10."

A trader who will not "consider" you, however, is no friend. Preferences to buy from friends and kinsmen, and actual purchases from such people, rest on strictly moral prescriptions only rarely. As one man observed: "The Krahn people, they will feel much happier to buy from a relative, because they think that when you buy from relatives the money is still in their reach. This sentiment is generalized to friends and is characteristic of urban consumers. 'Good customer' relations involve a balanced and brittle reciprocity on which there are clear bounds. Where traders do not fulfill customers' expectations, buyers simply look elsewhere for considerations."

Good customers are valued for the assurance of sales they imply in the long run. But good customers are unreliable sources of business in the short run. To avoid spoilage losses traders generally feel that they need to sell fast. There are some notable exceptions. If a trader has all her money tied up in stocks—as not infrequently she does—and/or cannot obtain supplemental stocks readily, she many choose to stay in the market all day trying to sell slowly, perhaps at a higher than average price. Furthermore, if a trader has a commitment to a good customer and no supplemental supplies, not infrequently, to preserve that relationship, she will refuse high prices offered her by others. But because any one intermediary has only a few such customers and consumers must spend their $1.00 daily allotment for food among many traders, sales to good customers can constitute only a small percentage of the sales necessary to make the trader's firm profitable. Moreover, the good customer relationship itself is grounded on the trader's offering the customer a low price. Consequently, traders point out that if adjustments in price are not made "people will not buy my goods," and "the money used for goods will not be made." Although personal networks are used to lessen competitive pressures somewhat, "good customer" relationships are grounded on competitive pricing. He who does not offer a good price from the buyer too often spoils the market and is no "good customer."

The only alternative to competitive price-making? "Carry your market to places where the people are plenty," and "purchase goods that are scarce"—that is, make spatial and temporal adjustments. For example, if you choose to sell from your house rather than from the marketplace, you could do quite well despite not offering consumers as wide a variety of food, prices as consistently low, or quality quite as high as those in marketplaces. You could make available small quantities of foods at times (Sundays, at night) when markets are closed, at places convenient for those wanting a small item not purchased at a market earlier in the day, and on terms (credit) available principally because seller and buyer are neighbors. Neighborhood sellers also offer a further advantage—shopping safety: when children have to shop, parents realistically worry about the dangerous traffic.

Just as traders ultimately are dependent on their firms for income, traders ultimately are dependent on their management ability to assure the viability of their firms. Risk is minimized most effectively and reliably by catering to the wants of consumers and producers. Although one need not initiate changes in price, to sell fast one must follow the lead of the unknown undercutter and take advantage of scarcity situations when they arise. Within established markets one must be sensitive to changing market conditions; alternatively, one must "take your market to where the people are plenty and the goods are scarce." Firms grow only where they can take advantage of new opportunities. Inefficient management results in business failure.

If you sell sex, firm management is simpler. To maintain your service supply you should protect your health and create a reliable set of regular customers. You should protect your health by consistently using condoms to reduce the risk of a sexually transmitted disease, and you should use frequent visits to health clinics to make sure you successfully avoid STDs. You should solidify a client base by offering regular customers discounted prices and by catering to unusual sexual requests—like oral sex, anal sex, multiple partners, various forms of sadomasochism, and fantasy sex.

Political Culture in Centralized Polities

Then my friend the Minister intervened . . . (Marris and Somerset, 1971: 197)

Business and politics share their central function—call it resource allocation, trade, commerce, or "scratch-my-back-and-I'll-scratch-yours." They go about it very differently, however. Political cultures consist of resources (of many, many kinds), people who have resources (patrons), and people who wish to have resources (clients). Political cultures, whether autocratic or theocratic, totalitarian or democratic, consist solely of patrons and clients. Patrons siphon resources from one set of people and allocate some of those resources to their clients. In the United States, the operational word for electoral constituents is *pork*. If a potential client wants access to those resources, he or she or it should provide patrons important services. Pork should yield votes, for example. The most important services extend the range of actions the patron may undertake with impunity, however. These more personal exchanges, which make the difference between patron and client fuzzier, might more accurately be characterized as *cronyism*.

Harold Lasswell nailed the essence of politics first, in 1936, when he published a book by that name and the subtitle *Who Gets What When and How*. In the early 1950s, David Easton retained Lasswell's definition of politics (albeit rewritten as *The Authoritative Allocation of Values*) even as his work helped revolutionize political science in the last half of the 20th century. Patrons exercise power. Clients do not. Patrons exercise power because their numbers aren't large. When the total number of patrons approximates no more than 7 +/−2, patrons tend to cooperate—at the expense of clients. Clients don't exercise power, because many, many clients compete with one another for the attention of the tiny number of patrons. Those engaged in political commerce who wish to maintain their positions, whether as patron or client, should suppress competitors while they reward clients. Growth in the number of patrons—growth, for example, in the number of food or sex retailers—balances the power of patrons and clients and makes it hard to tell who is patron and who is client. Patronage works the same wherever you go. I set my *Parable of the Good Son* in West Africa:

> Once upon a time there were three brothers by the same father and mother. They were born and reared in a farm village in the interior of Africa and were very close. They went through school together, moved to a large city and

shared lodging and, in their first jobs, all went to work for the same public agency. Here is how they differed:

In his first position, agricultural extension aide, [the second of the three brothers] found that several head of cattle and hogs died soon after they were delivered for him to distribute to farmers. He gave one cow to his supervisor to show gratitude for being hired as an aide and used the proceeds of the sale of the remaining meat to build a large house in his village. His parents moved into the house and rented out some of the rooms. When he was in charge of automobile procurement, he wrote two off on the official books as being beyond repair; he made one his own and sold the other to buy land near his village. When he was managing a division of the agricultural extension service, he discovered that some improved rice seed had spoiled and that several hundred rubber and coffee seedlings had been broken. Since he had shipped an earlier lot of cocoa seedlings to the farm of his Director, he planted these seeds and seedlings on his own farm. Because he could neither oversee the farm himself nor perform all the work, he appointed a cousin to manage it and hired people in the village to work on it. [After] he was appointed Assistant Minister for Development Planning... [he] brought brothers, sisters, and cousins to live with him, and he sent them to school. Later, he obtained government scholarships for them to attend college or to obtain postgraduate training abroad.

The first son enjoyed his job and worked hard, resisting all temptations to use his position to enrich himself. He was dedicated to the development of his country and, being a productive worker, he rose to be manager of a department of the Ministry of Finance. His family and friends, however, thought him a bit of a fool for not taking advantage of opportunities given by his positions. Or, maybe just naive. The third son, like the second son, used his positions to enrich himself and bought fancy clothes, cars, yachts, parties, girlfriends, and drugs. He ended with neither family nor friends. Narcissists accumulate clients only if they spread the wealth. (1987: 307–53)

Centralized political systems most plausibly arose, as Elman Service argued in his *Origins of the State and Civilization* (1975), when a person found a way to forcibly siphon resources from one set of people to reward a set of clients and thus transformed him- or herself into a patron. Clients formed patronage networks that we now call *bureaucracies* and receive rewards partly by collecting the resources (often called *taxes*) allocated to them by their patron. The patron, for his or her part, reserves some resources to enlarge the set of clients. Despite variation in the language used to talk about resource siphoning and the means to allocate resources to clients, you'll find it easy to find analogues of the second son in my parable globally—China, Afghanistan, Russia, England, Nicaragua, and Washington, DC. A Google search (as I write this) for "corruption in Afghanistan" pulls up more than 21,100,000 hits.

As an exercise, find the current net worth of current and recent national leaders. A quick example (h/t Wikipedia and ignoring the royal families): *billionaire* politicians include Saddam Hussein (Iraq), Silvio Berlusconi (Italy), Saad Hariri (Lebanon), Daniel Arap Moi (Kenya), Vladimir Putin (Russia), and Akbar Hashemi Rafsanjani (Iran); among those worth *at least* $10 million (but up to $900 million), count David Cameron (UK), Barack Obama (USA), Fidel Castro (Cuba), Yasser Arafat (Palestine), and former presidents G. W. Bush, G. H. W. Bush, and Bill Clinton (USA).

And before we go farther: I use the word *corruption* not to impute negative connotations to political culture but simply because it greatly eases the world wide web search for examples of patrons siphoning resources from one or another source to reward their clients. Participants in political cultures don't think of themselves as engaging in any sort of illegitimate activity. Indeed, they follow the cultural norms. You scratch my back and I'll scratch yours. Be loyal. Receive rewards. To do otherwise takes you beyond the moral code of the behavioral domain and will count as irresponsible, even dangerous behavior.

As I write this, Google produces 36,000,000 hits if you substitute Russia for Afghanistan. Google produces 62,000,000 hits if you substitute China for Russia. Closer to home, JoAnn Watson, a Detroit City Councilwoman, asked the President to bring home the bacon—by saving the city from bankruptcy—because Detroit overwhelmingly voted for his reelection. A study by the University of Illinois at Chicago and the University of Illinois Institute of Government and Public Policy finds that Chicago is the most corrupt city in the nation.

Exemplars abound that show laws are for the little people, not the connected. Compare, for example, the 2012 prosecution of David Gregory for knowingly violating D.C. law by exhibiting on national television a large-capacity magazine for an AR 15 clone with the prosecution of Iraq and Afghanistan veteran Adam Meckler for unknowingly violating D.C. law by forgetting that he had some cartridges in a backpack. Washington D.C.'s attorney general, a family acquaintance of Gregory, passed on the former and jailed the latter.

Public office corresponds with social networks, information, and opportunities that significantly enhance a Congressional Representative's chances of becoming a millionaire, for example. Senators enjoy still greater perks. The widely documented revolving door between even low-level government employment (as congressional aides, for instance) and lucrative postgovernment employment with lobbying firms and large corporations suggests that the U.S. government may lead the world in public sector corruption. In early September, 2014, Google produced only 36 million hits for Russia and 62 million hits for China but more than 74 billion hits for the United States. Tough competition for the top spot in the corruption racket.

However, America may lead the world in what has come to be known as *crony capitalism*. The large organizations to which regulations apply consistently write these regulations (although sometimes only indirectly via paid lobbyists). Regulations also create opportunities for graft and opportunities for advancement from, say, federal prosecutor, to corporate lawyer, to head of the Securities and Exchange Commission—in 2013, think Mary Jo White. This situation might explain why the District of Columbia, home of much poverty, reported a 2012 per capita income of $74,773—71% higher than the national average (http://www.bizjournals.com/washington/blog/2013/12/dc-far-out-paces-nation-in-personal.html).

Another useful exercise? Trace your own favorite exchanges among the political-economic elite. Does China's Politburo enrich themselves faster than American senators and members of Congress?

U.S. College Cultures Yield Parties

College students draw on many cultures as they seek academic certification, beyond the local variant of the world culture of Higher Ed. Let's call one of these a culture of Fun. The culture of Higher Ed tells students that colleges and universities exist to qualify graduates for admittance to a comfortable life (with prospects for more). The culture of Fun tells students that life is something to embrace and enjoy. Fun consists of things like people (with specific age, gender, and other characteristics) with whom to have fun, degrees of intimacy (stranger, acquaintance, friend, hookup, boy/girlfriend), places at which to have fun (dorm rooms, ballrooms, study-abroad beaches, and bars), means of having fun (parties, alcohol, other drugs, selecting easy classes rather than hard ones), fun behaviors (laughing, touching, kissing, drinking, teasing, holding hands, hugging, sex, visiting people with whom to have fun in dorm rooms, sorority houses, fraternity houses), and fun kinds of dress (shorts, short-shorts, short skirts, low-cut blouses, sexy bras, no bras). The central moral precept of this culture is that you should have fun.

How you go about that, however, varies with two other campus cultures, one of Entitlement and one of Accomplishment. The culture of Entitlement tells students that they deserve a college degree, that college years count as their last years without adult responsibility, and that they deserve to enjoy their last years of childhood—although no college student will use that phrase. Given that college years count as the last years without adult responsibilities and that individuals deserve to enjoy themselves, the students who participate in these cultures conclude that they should engage in as many fun activities as possible, as often as possible, without a thought about the hazards other people may see in these activities.

Although the proportion of students who participate in the culture of Entitlement seems to grow annually, campuses also contain students who participate in a culture of Accomplishment. This culture tells students that college is serious work that, if they take it seriously, may prepare them for an exciting, productive life. Serious students take college work as a set of adult responsibilities—to think about ideas, to engage ideas with faculty and other students, to actively participate in classes, to prepare for these discussions by completing assignments, and to manage their time so they can achieve all these things and have fun, too.

Cross-Domain Cultures

Cultures define activity domains, but some activity domains apply across behavioral domains like health care, retail sales, politics, and parties. The Entitlement culture described earlier counts as a very common such culture. The specifics apply to the specifics of the behavioral domain, whether college parties or the perks of patronage. But entitlement rests on the presumption that you possess an unalienable *right* to happiness—not-repeat-not the *pursuit* of happiness—even if other people do not.

Other cross-domain cultures tell us how to respond to norm violations. Thomas Sowell's *A Conflict of Visions* contains a wonderfully clear statement of two cultural postulates with enormous implications. One, which Sowell called the *unconstrained vision*, postulates that we can change human nature and make it better, even perfect. If you start from the unconstrained postulate that people are naturally good but, being human, make mistakes, you will conclude with the moral precept that you should help norm violators restore their innate good selves. The other, *constrained*, vision postulates that we cannot change human nature, which is inherently selfish. If you start from the constrained postulate that people will exploit you if they can and treat you well only if they must, you will conclude with the moral precept that you should defend yourself; punishments of varying kinds and severity count as important means of norm violation prevention.

Human minds come with the intuition that all people do things for reasons and that these are knowable. Cultures, however, tell us how we may know these reasons. If you start from the postulate that you cannot know what another person thinks unless you ask and recognize that even then the other may try to deceive, you should do your best to elicit clear explanations from the other's point of view. You should not accept explanatory stories unless you find a correspondence between the story and specific forms of observed behavior. If you start from the postulate that you can know what another person thinks without having to ask, you should not waste your time and energy trying to see the world from another point of view. External characteristics will tell you the right answer every time.

A fourth set of cross-domain culture works synergistically with the cultures that tell how to know why a person makes one choice or another and how you should respond to norm violations. One culture rests on the postulate that all humans come into the world with unalienable rights. The other rests on the postulate that no, or only some, humans come into the world with unalienable rights. Human activity at any time and place comes from the interaction of a set of domain- specific cultures. Change the set and you change activity dramatically.

Chapter 3

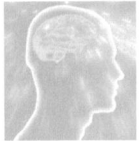

Morally Ordered Behavior Gives Cultures Agency

Stripped to its essence, combat is a series of quick decisions and rather precise actions carried out in concert with ten or twelve other men. In that sense it's much more like football than, say, like a gang fight. The unit that choreographs their actions best usually wins. They might take casualties, but they win.

That choreography—*you lay down fire while I run forward, then I cover you while you move your team up*—is so powerful that it can overcome enormous tactical deficits. There is a choreography for storming Omaha Beach, for taking out a pillbox bunker, and for surviving an L-shaped ambush at night on the Gatigal. The choreography always requires that each man make decisions based not on what's best for *him*, but on what's best for the . . . [culture]. If everyone does that, most of the group survives. If no one does, most of the group dies. That, in essence, is combat. (Junger, 2010: 120)

And that, in essence, is how cultures do things. People act on what best corresponds to the moral order for a specific behavioral domain.

In his 1952 book *The Uses of the Past*, Herbert Muller points out that the assumptions that rationalize the caste system of the Indian subcontinent, for example, deny the possibility of improving a living person's circumstances. The cultural assumption of an unchangeable reality and the ideals of renunciation of life and passivity preclude actions to improve the lives of anyone. These assumptions do not produce corruption, high death rates, and low life expectancies, but "if the temporal world is illusion there is no important difference between freedom and slavery, justice and injustice" (1952: 334). These assumptions give no one who belongs among their collective adherents moral superiority over another, but they inevitably produce indifference to suffering. Because they rationalize the life circumstances of people in the lowest walks of life and give all people deprived of social justice the opportunity of a better life next time around, they ensure the safety of those who occupy the highest caste ranks.

But they also produce vulnerability to unexpected change. Muller observes, by contrast, that:

> No drama in history is more fascinating than the rise of Yahweh. Starting out as an obscure deity of a despised people, apparently incapable of protecting them from their enemies, he nevertheless triumphed over his far more powerful rivals and eventually conquered a mighty civilization. Offhand, it is the very model of the success story—the story of a local god who made good, against terrific odds. And it is a story of character, not luck. (1952: 80)

Yahweh succeeded, Muller argues, because the Prophets

> evolved a more rational, responsible history than any other people had yet conceived. Instead of foisting history on Fate, they explained it by human character and conduct. The moral value of this conception of history is plain. It puts the issue squarely up to man, declaring his responsibility for good and evil. (1952: 92)

Judaic Prophets made possible adaptable and thriving communities in the Diaspora despite the population of adherents being "scattered over the face of the earth, despised, oppressed, persecuted, exposed to a martyrdom more cruel and prolonged than another people had had to endure" (1952: 94). How? Because they denounced injustice and insisted that Jews, individually and collectively, accept moral responsibility for social justice and injustice alike.

Cultures thus tell us the moral orders that apply to specific behavioral domains. When behavior corresponds to cultural norms, cultures act as agents and achieve goals.

What Does America's Oral Health Culture Do?

The health culture described in Chapter 2, for example, produces a national population with good to excellent oral health. It coerces good oral health by inducing embarrassment at not regularly visiting the dentist or not flossing regularly. Failure to act out cultural norms makes dental clients defensive. As one young woman in Connecticut noted: "I always know they'll give me a hard time about flossing, and I have no excuse so I feel stupid." Another felt her recent dental office visit went well and explained: "I wasn't yelled at for supposedly not flossing."

Fear of pain and invasive practices characteristic of dental health care deter dental visits. A person's embarrassment at having bad teeth provides a vital incentive to override the fear. But only if you participate in that oral health culture.

The meaning of things varies with your assumptions. Nearly everyone in America can describe the norms of the American oral health culture. To participate, however, you must postulate that appearance and having good teeth count as very important. If you don't, your behavior corresponds to the norms of another culture. "Looking good" does not, for example, affect the material well-being of men and women who move from job to job working at an all-night record store, in food delivery, as a factory or farm workman, or as a fast food cook and who find a mate among others who do likewise. If appearance doesn't matter, you shouldn't waste time and energy on oral health care and seek care only at the last resort. This culture provides the clients who show up at hospital ERs for emergency care and whose oral health practices dental providers find troublesome. They brush irregularly if at all and avoid dental visits until the pain gets too great. In the process, they may make dental appointments but cancel them if the pain abates or something more pressing comes up. The delay in addressing the problem makes their pain and the complexity of the health issue much worse. The cost of the dental procedures goes up in both time and money. An initial visit typically aims to reduce or eliminate the pain. Because these clients value no pain but do not value good teeth, the dental providers who do and who schedule follow-up procedures find themselves with further cancellations. This culture thus makes health care costs rise and rise and rise.

Dentistry practices appear in the archaeological record concurrently with the shift from foraging to farming. America's oral health culture, however, came into being as one outcome of the growth of a global economy.

The relative importance of appearance and having good teeth is a function of the cultural norms imposed on people who aspire to career tracks and increasingly responsible work or social positions in the global market economy. Good teeth reflect self-worth and discipline. After all, a man pointed out: "having brown teeth makes people think you don't take care of yourself." However terrified one might feel at the prospect of extensive dental work: "It was embarrassing. You could see the decay just by talking to me. It was visible, and some of the cavities were so big and so deep in front that you could see them when I smiled. 'J' said that it "looked like I had popcorn kernels stuck in my teeth."

Bad teeth, like warts or pimples, but far more important than either, count as a cosmetic problem—even to most dental providers. The commercial advertising of popular culture and print and broadcast media have it right that looking good improves a person's ability to enhance their material well-being and attract a mate. We not only know how to prevent dental disease; we regularly brush our teeth and visit a dental provider and make sure our children do, too. If we get a poor start, we catch up. Without exception, people who reported having had bad teeth earlier in life but good teeth now explained their change in oral health status by reference to a change in life circumstances. Earlier in their lives, appearance did not matter. Because of the jobs they held and their unconcern with social and economic mobility, even grossly unaesthetic decayed and missing teeth produced no effect worthy of notice. Later, it did, but only because they anticipated that a pleasing personal appearance—one that told your audience that you thought well enough about yourself to take care of yourself—would be necessary to achieve their new social and economic mobility goals.

Business Cultures: Selling Food, Selling Sex

Just as traders ultimately are dependent on their firms for income, traders ultimately are dependent on their management ability to assure the viability of their firms. A trading environment easy to enter produces competition. Competition eliminates collusion as a viable trading option and creates the cultural norm that sellers should find imaginative ways to satisfy their clients. Because entrepreneur-managers depend on their business for their livelihood, to optimize the amount and reliability of their income they should minimize the risk of business failure. To minimize the risk of business failure, entrepreneur-managers should initiate firms whose specific properties allow the profitable handling of commodities with given properties (for example, durable or perishable), and they should minimize or eliminate competition either by catering to sectors of population that other firms do not tend to or (if firms are serving the same sector of population) by catering to demands that other firms do not cover.

Because the effect of one or another system of ideas or behavioral patterns is relative to the material circumstances in which it emerges, in different technological systems and in different niches, this optimizing tendency must take different forms and will result in different marketing activities: firms with different properties conducting business at different periods of time, operating at different relative locations, and trading different lines of merchandise. Traders make decisions under uncertainty, and in retrospect some entrepreneur-managers make errors. Those who make better choices create a network of exchange sites and firm types whose service functions, spatial distribution, and work hours complement rather than conflict with one another. Changes in the constraint parameters with reference to which trading is carried out imply change in the relative efficiency of alternative preference structures and behavioral patterns, as well as changes in the relative efficiency of different kinds of firms, different kinds of exchange sites, and different spatiotemporal alignments of firms and exchange sites. Businesses successful at one point in time may falter at another. Thus, over time, selective processes generate trading networks whose components, functions, spatial distribution, and work hours adjust to changes in these constraint parameters.

In the second half of the 20th century, in Liberia these norms and these practices created a growing and spatially and temporally complementary network of exchange sites and firm types that created new income-earning opportunities for both farmers and city dwellers and improved nutrition and material life conditions for both. Trade in foodstuffs provided funds with which to send children through school, to regularly add meat and fish to the diet, to dress better, to enjoy the benefits of zinc-roofed houses rather than thatch. It added to global markets new flows of such commodities as rubber, coffee, cocoa, and palm kernels, which, owing to increasing global competition, lowered the costs to consumers while it improved the well-being of all Liberians.

In the second half of the 20th century, in Barbados the cultural norm that sellers should find imaginative ways to satisfy their clients produced (as in Liberia) a growing and spatially and temporally complementary network of exchange sites and firm types that created new income-earning opportunities and improved nutrition and material life conditions. Sex sales also contributed to the spread of HIV.

Ed Green points out in his 2011 book *Broken Promises* that the AIDS epidemic in Africa—and STDs more generally—would not exist if people delayed the onset of sexual activity and remained monogamous once they start. Sexually transmitted infections require multiple partners. Epidemics, however, require large-scale sexual precociousness and sexual mobility. Most dangerously, STD epidemics flare when both partners engage in multiple sexual contacts concurrently. Green's long-term research in Africa showed what should have been obvious—that initiating sexual activity late and sexual fidelity ("zero grazing") dramatically lower incidence rates of HIV.

Remember, however, that the meaning of something varies with one's assumptions. Green points out that, if you assume that your job is to identify practices that lessen or facilitate the spread of HIV, you should pay attention to the effects of plausible determinants and clearly describe their effects. If, however, you take for granted that cultural differences just make us different and that everyone has the right to find his or her own ways to enjoy sex even if that means starting sex early and maintaining concurrent sexual relations, the cognitive biases in your mind will make you see something very different. The same cognitive biases (Chapter 5) that led leaders in science to dismiss out of hand the (eventual) Nobel Prize winning work of Barbara McClintock (jumping genes), Stanley Prusiner (prions), and Dan Schechtman (quasi-crystals) will make you rule out the possibility of identifying core practices that lessen or facilitate the spread of HIV.

You will notice things that do not violate these assumptions. You probably will notice the evidence that circumcision inhibits the spread of HIV, which may further your confidence that barrier methods like condoms should be emphasized in intervention programs. You'll be puzzled, consequently, to find that HIV rates rise when condom use rates rise. Your cultural assumptions, however, will make you reject out of hand any suggestion that abstinence and sexual fidelity are relevant to HIV incidence rates despite evidence from Uganda of highly effective ABC intervention cultures (Abstinence, Be faithful, and—if you can't—use Condoms Consistently). Your cultural assumptions about moral relativity and sex will thus blind you to the possibility that, in Africa, condom use lowered the age at which people initiated sexual activity and increased concurrent sexual "grazing" without consistent safe-sex condom use. Repeated data collection showed that Africans consistently practiced less sexual mobility than Americans and Europeans. Your culture will make that observation difficult to recognize for what it says—that there's something beyond simple numbers of sexual partners that spreads HIV. Your culture will thus kill millions of Africans as it produces HIV incidence rates like 23% of the population aged 15–49 in Lesotho, 17% in South Africa, and 15% in Zimbabwe.

The choice-frame mechanism built into human minds gives individuals agency to go it alone when all their cognitive biases tell them to go along. Ladies of the evening in Barbados recognize that selling sex requires that you maintain a reliable service supply, that you should protect your health. They know that HIV kills you, which intensifies the importance of avoiding STDs. Consistent condom use helps significantly, so ladies should (and do) consistently use condoms. These cultural norms mean that, in the late 20th century, men, not "prostitutes" and "promiscuous" women, became the active STD transmitters in Barbados.

Condoms have been widely used on Barbados since the end of World War II. Virtually everybody knows about them, and nearly everybody has used them at least once. Today they are readily available. They are advertised in newspapers and can be found in small shops, groceries, and pharmacies throughout the island.

Condoms aren't popular. Women complain of chafing, rashes, and the absence of "good sensations." Both men and women complain that condoms may burst. Men complain that they lose sensitivity and so lose their erection, or they take an inordinate amount of time to orgasm. Some men still declare that "Condoms will never be accepted on Barbados!" and "I would never use a condom; I'd rather jerk off than wear a condom, and I've done so on more than one occasion!" The same men also usually still deny that AIDS is a disease with which people should concern themselves.

Who doesn't use condoms? Men, unless they're forced to, and women who believe they're part of a monogamous union. In a national survey undertaken in 1990, about half the sample of women thought their partners were sexually monogamous. However, 7 out of 10 men reported that, in fact, they had sex with women other than their current partner. Not surprisingly, 38% of the women who said that they prevented disease by staying with one partner reported a history of STDs.

By contrast, men's condom use constitutes an empowering strategy. The reasons men give for not using condoms don't reveal this. Men, like women, usually say they use condoms when they fear disease, as with a lady of the evening, or a new partner they don't know well. In fact, however, the men who don't use condoms are those who believe themselves physically and emotionally abused as a child by their mother. There existed too few cases of men sexually abused as children to clearly establish childhood sexual abuse as a condom-use predictor, but I suspect more data would confirm this possibility.

Family violence thus has shaped both concepts of sexuality and sexual behavior in ways that encourage the spread of sexually transmitted diseases. The population of women who sell sexual services harbors a pool of transmissible pathogens. But it is not by their choice. Barbadian men historically have demanded "flesh-to-flesh" contact.

Whereas women usually loathe even the thought of contracting an STD, men tend to accept STDs as a minor risk of "macho" activities, much as the German aristocracy accepted dueling scars. Thus, Barbadian men, particularly susceptible to HIV transmission because few are circumcised, spread the pathogens from girlfriend to wife (rarely to ladies) and back again. Men most likely to spread STDs are those who were physically, emotionally, and/or sexually abused as children and who, consequently, have many sexual partners and don't use condoms.

Ladies of the evening, by contrast, have come to carry their own condoms and, when asked, correctly show how and when to use it, and how to discard it safely. One client said it best: "The ladies are very, very scared. Mostly they won't let you have sex with them without a condom. Even if they suck you, they want a condom." As of the last decade of the 20th century, every experienced lady and every client told me the same story. Ladies do not sell sex without condoms. The HIV incidence rate in Barbados of around 1.5% as of 2012 may be explained by the ladies who actively inhibit the spread of HIV. This rate won't fall into the lowest 0.1–0.2% rates, however, until the rate of concurrent and risky sexual networking falls. This change probably requires a shift to the ABC culture.

Political Culture in Centralized Polities

A fish rots from the head. (Kru Proverb)

Power corrupts, and absolute power corrupts absolutely. (Lord Acton)

Political cultures, to reiterate, consist of resources (of many, many kinds), people who have resources (patrons), and people who wish to have resources (clients). Patrons siphon resources from one set of people and allocate some of those resources to their clients. In return, clients increase the range of actions that patrons may perform with impunity. Clients must find ways to attract the attention of patrons. Indeed, they compete among themselves win favor with potential patrons. The effects of political cultures vary by the extent to which resource allocation occurs solely via patron-client exchanges.

In Africa, the industrial system brought with it new income-earning opportunities, redefined work competences in terms of the schooling and technical training necessary to operate the new technologies, and implied the expanded use of money. People who were knowledgeable and skilled farmers were transformed into illiterate, unskilled men and women who were only marginally employable in the industrial system. Educational attainment and skill training became avenues through which a new resource, money, could be obtained in quantity. Money itself came to be necessary for subsistence. The use of money for subsistence and the differential access to money implicit in the industrial system created socioeconomic differences that did not exist in precolonial Africa.

But Africa's integration into the world system occurred in a context in which access to education, jobs, and income was channeled almost solely through the colonial system. As mentioned earlier, since early in the 20th century there have been few employment opportunities for Africans in firms run by expatriates, and Africa's best and brightest have opted for civil service employment rather than entrepreneurship. The reason is simple: colonial governments were making it almost impossible for African entrepreneurs to run profitable businesses, but they were paying their African civil servants relatively (for Africans) high salaries. Moreover, public sector employment facilitated access to capital that could be used to carry out the low-level entrepreneurial functions that were left open to Africans. This situation worsened in the postcolonial period. African entrepreneurship as well as employment in managerial positions in expatriate firms is more closely tied to political patronage now than it ever was during colonial rule.

This centralization of power is a legacy of the colonial period when European nations created state political structures in Africa to administer rather than to serve and appropriated to themselves control over the resources of the emerging world industrial system. As Elliot Berg points out, and as Peter Bauer documented in detail, when African states achieved independence they had behind them "a half-century of history cluttered with memories of price-fixing arrangements, government-bestowed monopoly privileges, restrictive wage and labor market policies, forced labor—all dependent on an alliance between colonial governments and private (almost exclusively foreign) enterprises" (1954: 26).

Newly independent African governments merely took over the single-channel resource structure that had been created by the colonial powers, which has continued to allow those who control government, who are almost solely men, to control access to the resources of the world industrial system. This gave them immense power, restricted the expansion of individual freedoms, and stressed the importance of properly managing personal relationships with the powerful, not of technical competence.

Corruption called by any name, however, leads to massive inefficiencies, misdirections of resources, public cynicism and mistrust of government, cynical and demoralized public employees, and uncoordinated or ungrounded public policy decisions that slow the process of economic growth and development. Entrepreneurs the world over depend on social relations based on mutual give-and-take to create, take advantage of, and expand on the opportunities that they see. In Africa, access to public sector clientage largely dictates who undertakes what kind of entrepreneurial activity and how they go about it. Few men and almost no women have important public sector patrons. Only those who do can reasonably expect to obtain high-level managerial experience in expatriate firms or to engage in large-scale entrepreneurship.

Public sector corruption thus has profound effects in the private sector. The least important of these are increased overhead costs due to money, gifts, and services that need to be proffered to patrons and prospective patrons. The subsequent regulatory environment not only requires many direct contacts with government officials but also systematically discriminates against small firms and operates in terms of unwritten rules that change every time a civil servant or office holder changes his or (rarely) her clientage network, and every time new appointments are made. Capital and labor market policies close off opportunities to small firms, and, for firms of all sizes, information costs are extraordinarily high in both time and money. Even in the best of circumstances, consequently, entrepreneurs recognize that valuable clientage ties to the public sector may evaporate without notice. It is this environment that makes it that much more imperative to maintain a clientage network that is as diverse as possible. Ties to family members and friends outside the public sector retain an importance that they would not otherwise have. It is this environment that also makes quick profits and diversification a far more important goal than sustained growth of a single firm based on long-term investments. Government employees inclined to pursue their own interests, including outside, private sector employment, generally find that it is easy to do so. Indeed, government employment provides access to capital in ways that no other employment does. Few high government officials forego the opportunity to use government resources for their own purposes. The more farsighted have developed their own business enterprises. Indeed, government-sponsored programs to develop indigenous entrepreneurship have primarily been tools for civil servants and public office holders to diversify their own economic holdings.

These practices, of course, merely illustrate the effects of a political culture that, in late 20th century Africa:

- Created a new ruling political class based on the intersection of clientage networks of government officials, entrepreneurs, and multinational firm leadership.
- Established that class membership and social mobility have less to do with technical competence than clientage, which unduly increases the proportion of firms that are not well run.
- Supported clientage networks that shelter these firms while they discourage and, frequently, penalize entrepreneurs who have the potential to create efficient, growing firms.

Sounds like early 21st-century U.S.A. (see, for example, Gilens and Page's "Testing Theories of American Politics" [2014]).

The global economy still reels from patron-client relationships run amok. Gillian Tett's 2009 book *Fool's Gold* focuses on a key foundation—the inclusion of subprime loans in the credit derivative markets. The book's advertising says it tells the story of how Wall Street greed corrupted a bold dream. Tett's account provides a clear view of the cultural dynamics that contributed to the global economic crisis of 2008. Like most ethnographies, however, the first write-up tends to be too narrowly focused. The problem (h/t Thayer Watkins) originated in 1938 with the formation of a government-sponsored enterprise (GSE), originally Fannie Mae and joined later by Freddie Mac, with the power to borrow directly from the U.S. Treasury and reward a set of clients.

Inclusion of subprime loans in the credit derivative markets occurred because lenders were required to take on unreasonable risk. The Community Reinvestment Act of 1977, for example, required banks to provide credit for people with poor credit. By the 1990s, these GSEs required banks to meet a quota of "subprime" loans—loans that were unlikely to be repaid—on the understanding that the banks would sell these mortgages to the GSEs. This increase in risk added to the incentive that banks had to create credit derivatives, in which seller A agrees to compensate buyer B if B is confronted by a defaulted loan. It would have been irresponsible for them to not pursue means to minimize the risk of business failure.

The GSEs protected themselves from oversight by heavily investing in patrons on the Senate Banking Committee—for example, Chris Dodd and Barney Frank. SBC members also profited by services like low-interest loan programs such as "Friends of Angelo," whose Countrywide lending operation made heavy profits from making the bad loans purchased by the GSEs. Tett's conclusion that "what is needed is a return to the seemingly dull virtues of prudence, moderation, balance, and common sense" makes perfect sense. We sometimes forget that our minds evolved a mechanism to tell us when we make mistakes; we call these things consequences. Humans cannot know they make a mistake if significant consequences don't tell them. Like the AIDS establishment culture that killed millions of Africans, the choices made by financial sector decision makers corresponded to a culture that told them the right thing to do—to reward constituents, to protect each other,

Business sales tell us that the level of patron-client exchange in the allocation of resources varies with the ease with which an individual can pursue a new opportunity to create wealth. If clients find easy entrance to many opportunities, patrons face lots of competition, because clients tend to support the patron who helps the most at the lowest cost. Just like the competition faced by Liberian market sellers and Bajan ladies of the evening. In today's world, patrons favor regulations—laws, certifications, and other enforceable rules. The more the better, because the ability to attract clients grows dramatically as the number of rules increases. In Liberia in the late 20th century, high school students had to use specific kinds of blue books for tests. Teachers sold the blue books. In the United States in the early 21st century, members of the congress and senate voted for an Affordable Care Act that required U.S. citizens to engage in a specific set of activities at specific times to acquire health insurance or to face specific sanctions otherwise. Members of the congress and senate, along with selected other clients, have been absolved from having to follow these rules. Patrons say to whom the regulations apply and may absolve clients from particularly onerous rule applications. Patrons even knowingly promise falsehoods.

The greater the power of patrons the harder it is to reverse the process that leads to even greater resource allocation levels via patronage. Most commonly, the process is brought to a halt by dramatic and traumatic violence as the patron-client system collapses—for example, the coup in Liberia that overthrew the previous regime and led to internal war that has only now stopped, and the collapse of the Soviet Union. China, thus far, has avoided collapse.

Reversal of power centralization becomes harder because the people with power, like all people, use minds that respond to the absence of consequences with the belief that they deserve their benefits. Powerful people thus fight increasingly harder to keep and extend the range of activities that produce no adverse consequences. Power corrupts because our minds come with biases that rationalize away things we know are wrong. Laws are for the little people. Not for the powerful. Power thus creates its own culture—of Entitlement. Clients form integral parts of political cultures, and they, too, deserve protection. The best way for clients to protect themselves, of course, is to provide cover for their patron if/when someone objects to the patron's actions. Joel Kotkin's essay "Watch What You Say, . . ." (2014b) nicely characterizes the dominant set of cronies in contemporary America.

Our minds evolved a set of biases that produces these changes in the minds of clients, like those of their patrons, not consciously but automatically. You'll see *why* our minds make these changes in Chapter 6. Here's a hint: "When we climb the ladder of status, our inner arguments get warped and our natural sympathy for others is vanquished. Instead of fretting about the effects of our actions, we just go ahead and act. We deserve what we want. And how dare they resist. Don't they know who we are?" (Lehrer 2011).

Meanwhile, note that the normal operation of human minds means that conventional political labels (Left, Right, Communist, Fascist, Republican, Democrat, Liberal, Conservative, Progressive, Libertarian) tell us nothing of importance. Neither does information about wealth inequalities. What is important? Maybe only your answer to these questions—Who among the politico-economic elite seeks more power, and do you hand it over or say "No!"? Wealth inequalities—like those enjoyed by the Barbadian agro-commercial elite through the first half of the 20th century—undercut politico-economic elites when they counter cronyism, as they did during the second half of the 20th century. I summarize in *Women's Power and Social Evolution*:

> [After mid-century] economic well-being of the Barbadian elite was increasingly subject to selection on the basis of quality and cost factors set in international markets. New firms were established on the island. Some of these have been extensions of multinational corporations, some have been extensions of Barbados Shipping and Trading, some have been established by new emigrants to Barbados, and others have been established on the basis of indigenous, nonelite (and nonwhite) entrepreneurship. The establishment of these firms created new resource access opportunities for the Barbadian population and, consequently, undermined the gatekeeper position of the agro-commercial elite. An island with an immense lower class was transformed into an island with an immense middle class. (1989: 96)

U.S. College Cultures Yield Party Outcomes That Vary Dramatically

The culture of Fun yields parties for participants in both the culture of Entitlement and the culture of Accomplishment. Party outcomes differ dramatically.

Participants in the culture of Entitlement get there by virtue of discovering that the range of things they can do without consequence is very large. They have power—though few if any young people think of it in those terms. They don't face consequences. Students who participate in the culture of Accomplishment, for example, get there by virtue of discovering that most actions have consequences, frequently tough ones. Poor writing, little effort on exams, failure to read assignments, to think about issues raised in the course, or to participate in class discussions resulted in harsh penalties. Because these students found that that you get only what you work hard for, it never occurs to attribute their successes or failures to anyone but themselves. If a student in the Accomplishment culture doesn't understand lecture material, he or she asks questions. If the instructor doesn't respond well, those students demand better responses. If students in the Accomplishment culture receive a poor evaluation of their writing, they ask for specific suggestions so they may improve. If students receive a poor response to or no suggestions for their writing, they may feel anger, but they work it out themselves. Students in the Accomplishment culture usually enjoy class material that explores how class material may apply to a host of issues beyond the exam. If such students were embarrassed by being singled out in class discussions for which they were ill-prepared, they prepare better for future classes. Students in the Entitlement culture, by contrast, feel offended when they get to college and find that their instructor grades their writing poorly, doesn't use PowerPoint slides to illustrate class materials, expects them to ask questions if they don't understand lecture, fails to limit class discussions or lectures to material that will be on the exam, and doesn't make the class exciting, and they find it "nerve wracking to be in lecture and not know what challenging question he may ask you next that you don't know how to answer." Because they think of themselves as consumers, and consumers know best, it never occurs to them to think about how their actions contribute to their own failure or success.

Participants in the two cultures approach fun dramatically differently, because their sense of entitlement or lack of entitlement has conditioned their take on cross-domain cultures that tell us how to respond to norm violations, how we may know the reasons people do things, and whether or not all or only some humans come into the world with unalienable rights.

Entitlement culture students conclude that they deserve the best because they're special (with no understanding of having achieved important goals) and that they deserve respect for being special. There's no need to be attuned to signals that someone may not treat them with respect. After all, if you're special, others *will* show you respect and *will* treat you well. Entitlement culture students become members of this culture because their experience tells them that yes, they occasionally make mistakes. But they're naturally good. The people who have assured them that they are special were careful to reassure these students that they were good people who just make human mistakes. Rather than impose punishments, these people did as the culture told them they should do: they helped the norm violator understand his or her mistake, so he or she could be restored to a sense of specialness. Entitlement culture students thus tend to assume the postulate that you can know what another person thinks without having to ask. External characteristics—particularly those that correspond with the characteristics that make you special—will tell you the right answer every time.

Accomplishment culture students, who conclude that they get only what they work hard for, party with the understanding that they have achieved important goals, that they deserve respect for those achievements, and so they remain attuned to signals that someone may not treat them with respect, indeed that people will exploit them if they can. Students who start from this postulate, who remain attuned to signals of mistreatment, adhere to the moral corollary that, given mistreatment, one should defend oneself; punishments of varying kinds and severity count as important means of norm violation prevention. They know, correspondingly, that you cannot know what another person thinks unless you ask and recognize that even then the other may try to deceive, so you should do your best to elicit clear explanations from the other's point of view. You should not accept explanatory stories unless you find a correspondence between the story and specific forms of observed behavior. Accomplishment culture students thus also tend to accept the postulate that all humans come into the world with unalienable rights. These rights include the right to "Life, Liberty, and the Pursuit of Happiness," although no student is likely to use these words.

Entitlement culture students, by contrast, are highly unlikely to have given any thought to the issue of rights.

Accomplishment culture students party heartily sometimes and enjoy themselves. Entitlement culture students, by contrast, party heartily often and enjoy themselves—until a cultural clash provides a comeuppance. To see a hint why, look, for example, at photographs of college parties posted on sites like The Chive (http://thechive.com/). Viewers who see them through a lens created by Entitlement culture laugh, ooh-and-ahhh, and comment "how cool!" Viewers who see the same photos through a lens created by another assumption may find themselves stunned by their offensiveness. A particularly striking recent photo shows a girl drinking beer held in a container that a boy holds behind his back, through a tube that passes between his legs. By one assumption you will see fellatio, mock or real. Change your assumption and you will see some lighthearted and exciting fun! The behavior captured in the photograph expresses teasing, pushing borders, working out one's self-esteem, exploring new things and feelings, and flirting. It's not really about sex at all.

Well, maybe it is. But that depends on your assumptions. What counts as a sexual invitation? How can you know? We'll return to questions like these in the last chapter.

If you party in ways that blend attire and drugs and drink and narcissistic impulses in ways that incapacitate, at rates that grow with the size of the Entitlement culture on campus, you will probably find yourself raped or subject to rape accusations. As the student complainant in the recent University of Montana quarterback rape trial said in a text message to her roommate: "Omg . . . I think I might have just gotten raped."

"I think I might have just gotten raped"?

What assumptions produce this kind of confusion? The confusion, Danielle Wozniak points out, comes from a form of learned helplessness. Why? One of her colleagues, Christine Fiori, suggests—correctly, I suspect—that learned helplessness comes as a natural consequence of a youth so sheltered that life experiences never required some college students to define who and what they are and why.

No one acts wrongly. Everyone conforms with cultural norms. Cultural clashes may, nonetheless and with much ambiguity, yield unwanted outcomes—"oafish hookup melodramas," as Camille Paglia so aptly calls them (http://time.com/3444749/camille-paglia-the-modern-campus-cannot-comprehend-evil/).

Chapter 4

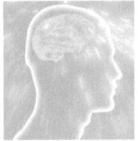

Living Requires Many Cultures, Thriving Requires They Be Well-Designed

Because cultures correspond to specific behavioral domains, we can't help but employ many, many cultures to live our lives. You, the reader, have almost certainly participated in the global culture of higher education, in at least one of the cultures that tell us how to respond to norm violations (people are born good, or not), in at least one of the cultures that tell us how to treat other people (people are born with unalienable rights, or not), and cultures that apply to families, sports teams, employment, friendship, intimacy, privacy, and commerce, whether involving food, sex, or something else.

Communities, too, reply on multiple cultures. We now know, for example, that the list of postulates that Hoebel used to describe Eskimo culture hold also for the !Kung, Pygmies, Australian Aborigines, Great Basin Shoshone, Hadza, Anishinaabe, and other foragers throughout the world. Three postulates about existential threats yield corollary cultural norms that explain how foragers manage to thrive, not merely survive: *The World Is a Dangerous Place, You Can't Survive on Your Own, and Family Is Most Reliable.*

What Could Be Dangerous?

Our understanding of violence in the lives of our ancestors has changed dramatically over time, shifting back and forth between imaginary positions stated most coherently by 17th-century thinkers Thomas Hobbes and Jean-Jacques Rousseau. Hobbes proposed that life among early humans was best characterized as "solitary, poor, nasty, brutish, and short." Rousseau proposed, by contrast, that life among early humans was best characterized as warm and gentle, egalitarian, and with morals unspoiled by civilization. We're still hashing things out. In the archaeological record we see widespread evidence of rape and dismemberment and death from violence, disease, and starvation. In these dangers, at least, our ancestors 100,000 years ago faced problems that we haven't escaped.

They, like us, drew on an accumulating intellectual capital in the form of increasingly sophisticated knowledge of regional food sources. Their descendants eventually used these bodies of knowledge about the growth characteristics and life cycles of their food sources to domesticate plants and animals. Long before this, however, our ancestors used this knowledge to design and employ a variety of capital goods such as nets, traps, bows, arrows, arrow points, spears, digging sticks, knives, axes, and poisons to acquire, harvest, and prepare food. The aim: a reliable flow of food all year.

Our ancestors ate the proverbial roots, berries, and nuts to the extent to which climate and season allowed. Mongongo nuts constituted up to 50% of the !Kung San diet, for example; up to 80% of their diet consisted of vegetable foods. Great Basin Shoshone starved when they failed to harvest 1,000 pounds or more of pine nuts to last them through the winter. Residents of the Arctic (Chukchi, Aleuts, Inupiat and Yupik Eskimo, Athabaskan peoples, among others) and places such as Tierra del Fuego (Yahgan) and northern Japan (Ainu), where roots, berries, melons, and nuts are few and far between, depended, of course, almost solely on meat and fish.

But everyone needs meat. Sometime well before our move out of Africa some 70,000 years ago, our ancestors lost the genes to construct all amino acids from scratch. Because we need amino acids to construct the proteins that build and run our bodies, we have to consume the "essential" amino acids as whole molecules. Ancestral health thus depended heavily on such foods as salmon, flounder, whale, seal, deer, walrus, antelope, crab, sardines, lobster, clams and mussels, boar, grubs, goats, sheep, insects, rabbits, and warthogs—which and in what quantity varied with location on the planet, season, temperature, precipitation, vegetation, and the level of previous hunting pressure by humans and other predators. The general availability of these food sources explains why studies of the San reveal very high levels of physical well-being, and the absence of these food sources explains why historical accounts from the Great Basin frequently report starving native populations.

Foragers took for granted that humans exert no meaningful control over the location or timing of their food supply. Because the world changes unexpectedly and sometimes very rapidly, neither variable can be predicted with much precision. It may take days, or longer, for a seal to appear at a breathing hole in the Arctic ice. When it does, the hunter may have to compete with a hungry Polar Bear. Caribou travel north over the tundra by routes that vary year to year. Pine trees produce nuts only once every three or four years, and productive regions in North America's Great Basin change from year to year. Whales may migrate past specific points of land each year, but times vary. Local weather, season, and climate may radically change game movements or delay the availability of plant foods.

Uncertainty of supply based on environmental variation added to uncertainties based on the physical dangers of hunting and collecting. Threats posed by predators after the same game, whether bears or leopards, crocodiles or wolves, or the threat posed by medium to large game who defend themselves aggressively with horns and hoofs, probably counted as minor problems. Far more important threats come from banal acts. A step in the wrong place may wrench an ankle and make it impossible to track game, much less to return to camp. A slightly different step may produce a spill that breaks a limb, or a neck. Or place you in range of a venomous snake, scorpion, spider, fish, or insect.

To borrow a phrase, the most dangerous game—our fellow people—posed the greatest threat. We have mediocre data on contemporary violence rates, awful data on violence rates a century or two earlier, and they only get worse the farther back in time we go. Contemporary claims about the relative violence rates at different places and times and how violence may or may not have changed rest on sand, or, a still better metaphor, on ice cream in the mid-summer sun. The problems start with the most fundamental issue: how should we measure violence?

Most contemporary measures express violence as rates per 100,000 population. We don't have data from prehistoric sites that can yet be reliably expressed in those terms. If we count the remains of people who clearly died by violence, we find that anywhere from 15% to more than 50% of all deaths came from violence. Mortality data from Arizona City in 1870, at 35%, fall into the middle of this range. Mortality data for the Russian Far East in the late 20th century fall at the extreme: 50% of all deaths, of men, come from violence. Rates vary over time and place, of course. The comparative data now suggest that "The Harmless People"—the !Kung San, so characterized by Lorna Marshall—had a death-by-violence rate of about 29.3/100,000 during the mid-20th century. Among the Hiwi in Colombia and Venezuela, the comparable rate immediately before contact was more than 1,000/100,000.

On the one hand, it's not obvious what should count as "violence" for comparative purposes or what should count as the population base. If we restrict ourselves to homicide deaths and compare the San with contemporary countries, we find that San violent death rates (29.3) were dramatically higher than those, for example, of the USA in 2010 (4.2). On other hand, they're comparable to the Central African Republic (29.3), South Africa (31.8), and much lower than the U.S. Virgin Islands (39.2) and Latin American countries now plagued by the drug trade, for example, El Salvador (69.2) and Honduras (91.6).

Perhaps, too, communities rather than countries should count as the population unit for comparisons like these? Some communities have very low rates of murder rates. El Paso, Texas, currently shows a rate of only 2.4. Cape Town's current murder rate, by contrast, is 62, and New Orleans, Louisiana, has sported murder rates of 50–60 over the past few years. The latest murder rate for New York City is 6.3, but, across the river, Newark's murder rate is 33.8.

More important still, these rates do not control for deaths averted by improved health care and by the Col. Colt effect—as in the popular post-Civil War slogan, "Abraham Lincoln May have Freed All Men, but Samuel Colt Made Them Equal."

However, total violence rates are dramatically higher. Only 22 deaths occurred from violent acts, but Richard Lee (1968) counted 81 acts of violence over the course of 50 years in a population of 1,500. Twenty-two deaths produce a murder rate of 29.3, but 81 acts produce a violence (violent crime) rate of 108/100,000 (compared, say, to a rate of 2,034/100,000 for the United Kingdom and 404/100,000 for the United States).

On still another hand, the rate of 108 does not count rapes, robberies, abductions, or the simple assaults that go into most 21st-century violent crime estimates.

And, in addition, dramatic variation may count as by far the most instructive feature of violence rates. In Wellington, Florida, the violence rate in 2010 was about 221. In Bonner's Ferry, Idaho, it was only 157. Washington, D.C., however, experienced a rate of 1,241—joined, at rates over 1,000, by such cities as Oakland, California; Miami, Florida; Albany, New York; St. Louis, Missouri; Chicago, Illinois; New Haven, Bridgeport, Hartford, and New London, Connecticut; and Chelsea, Springfield, New Bedford, Fall River, Holyoke, Brockton, and Lowell, Massachusetts. By contrast, Austin, Texas, experienced a rate of only 476, Portland, Oregon, a rate of only 541, and, across the Columbia River, Vancouver, Washington, only 401. Camden, New Jersey, however, experienced a violence rate greater than the United Kingdom, and three adjacent communities in Illinois just across the Mississippi River from St. Louis, Missouri, averaged around 6,000 acts of violence per 100,000 people. To complicate matters still further, violent crime rates vary dramatically by specific neighborhoods.

Neighborhoodscout.com reports that in 2013 one neighborhood in Detroit counted as the most violent in the nation, with a rate of 14,948 acts of violence per 100,000. A neighborhood in Chicago came in below two additional Detroit neighborhoods at #4, with a rate of 11,656 acts of violence per 100,000.

An aim to better understand what produces violence will likely yield more useful findings than attempts to characterize our ancestors as more or less violent than we are. On the one hand, we have accounts from Australia, Native North America, and the South Pacific of highly ritualized "wars" that attract audiences and in which people rarely die, because they effectively dodge incoming arrows or spears. On the other, to judge from the patterns among 20th-century foragers, serious violence erupts when men fight over women and rights to children, and when men seek to avenge the death of a friend or family member. In short: why fight? To defend yourself. The emergence of centralized polities brought with it the phenomenon we call *war* and a new way to talk about the application of violence: national defense. That changed nothing. Why fight? —to defend your women and your children and to avenge the death of a friend or family member.

Moreover, You Can't Survive on Your Own

"Because you can't" produces a moral vision in which
- you should form reliable ties with other people and live close to them;

- you should rely on instrumental criteria when you make judgments about yourself and the people you live with.

Because people vary in what they do well,

- you should assign tasks and activities according to abilities and aptitudes, in ways that
- produce coordination among those tasks and activities, in ways that
- enhance the chances of survival among the cooperating set of people by sharing the output of each person's assigned task and activity.

By far the most prevalent division of labor assigned men the tasks of hunting, defense, and maker of tools and shelter; women the tasks of childbearing, gathering, care of the young and aged, and food storage and preparation; older men and women less strenuous tasks based on the adult division of labor; and children either no responsibilities or supervisory responsibilities over younger siblings that increased as the siblings grew older. Adults thus were charged with the productive tasks of defense and food acquisition and distribution, by which to care for elderly and subadult family members. Elders contributed perspective and knowledge and the ability to substitute for adults in immediate subsistence activities. Children grew into adults who cared for the adults who grew old, and who shifted their activities from defense and food acquisition and distribution to supplemental assistance for children-turned-into-adults.

Don't Tell Me What to Do

But because (as Hoebel summarized) life is hard and the margin for safety small, when you are doing all of this—creating an interdependent division of labor that yields safety for all, including creating ways to enforce norms—you should not impose constraints on individuals that make life harder and reduce that margin for safety. Foragers characteristically translate this rule into two more specific corollaries:

- Individuals should be subject to minimal constraints or directives.
- Individuals should have a say in the constraints that apply to their behavior.

These moral precepts rule out centralized authorities, fixed forms of property, rigid rules of camp membership, and judgments reliant on imaginary effects, skills, or accomplishments. Foragers consistently apply utilitarian criteria to tasks of living and apply clear criteria to distinguish real from imaginary threats to their well-being.

Because a division of labor creates a web of mutual dependencies, relationships among community members are roughly egalitarian. Relative dependencies vary with the contributions of men and women and with the specific contributions of specific people. Skills in hunting, tool making, decision making, dispute resolution, planning, negotiation, and other critical activities bring admiration and respect. The much-studied !Kung San of the Kalahari have a formal position of "headman." This position carries with it no more authority, however, than the headman's demonstrated leadership competence.

But respect depends on mutual respect—and mutual dependence. For example, a common moral corollary states that individuals should have access to the available resources unrestricted by anything other than their personal choices and actions. On the one hand, individuals should use implements of production (capital goods) as much as possible. On the other, if they don't use it, they should let others use it. Similarly, individuals should claim only the resources and capital goods (implements of production) they can actually use. Foragers thus don't assert exclusive property claims. Men generally received more respect than women because they provide meat. Where the contributions of women to the food supply is relatively low, as among North Alaskan Eskimo, women experience a far lower status than places where women contribute huge amounts of energy and nutrients, such as among the San.

Two further corollaries follow:

- Groups should exhibit minimal rules of membership.
- Groups should exhibit maximal rules of affiliation.

Foragers lived in camps consisting of mobile or temporary shelters—with a few exceptions. Individuals should be free to shift locations depending on relative productivity, however. San foragers thus concentrate around permanent water holes during the dry season and shift to small camps that move widely once the rains fall again. Shoshone moved to pine nut groves in the fall. Copper Eskimo move onto the ice, once the Arctic Ocean freezes, to hunt seals. They shift to fish as the ice melts and, in the summer, disperse south to intercept caribou that move north. Whale hunts are most safely carried out with large groups. North Alaskan Eskimo (Inupiat) established large permanent village places that made possible effective spring whale hunts—at Point Hope, Icy Cape, Ukpiarvik, and Point Barrow. After the annual migration of whales passed, they moved into smaller seal hunting camps and, once the sea ice had departed in mid-summer, dispersed even more to fish and hunt caribou.

Camps with better hunters grow large. Specific technologies—-hunts that rely on driving game ahead of a half-circle of nets a hundred yards (or a mile) wide—call for larger camps. Other technologies—hunting individual food animals with bows and arrows—call for a more dispersed population and smaller camps.

Moreover, Don't Add to Our Uncertainties

Given that individual well-being required that one person help another, individuals should act predictably (that is, follow cultural norms). Violation of this norm threatened not merely specific people but the viability of the entire community. An individual who violated group norms was subject to a variety of forms of intervention, including becoming subject to ridicule and various forms of criticism, including simple avoidance of the person's company. Moving away to form a new camp counted as a common tactic to maintain camp viability.

Violence replaced nonviolent interventions when the latter failed to restore cooperative behavior. Because lack of cooperation threatens the well-being of all camp residents, people who failed to maintain group norms of cooperation and sharing:

> should either not be supported or simply eliminated,
> either by exile or execution.

Communities ordinarily sanctioned the execution of men who kill others readily—/Twi and ≠Gau among the !Kung, and Padlu among the Central Inuit, to name only a few of the well-known cases. If you attack another, you should anticipate being attacked. Qijuk, an Inuit, stole the wife of Kinger while the latter was out hunting. Kinger killed Qijuk in response. His friends and family attacked and killed one of Qijuk's two brothers, who had helped with the initial theft.

So, who can you count on when you need help?

Family Is Most Reliable

The most immediate corollary states that you should organize yourselves into family groups that coordinate their behavior for the benefit of all (that is, teams). Human imagination has come up with many, many ways to do this. One constant is that the core unit consists of a things we call husband, wife, and children. However, what counts as a husband, a wife, or a child varies. Ghosts, women, and whole villages may count as husbands. Females most commonly count as wives, but many American Indian communities recognized two-spirit people who, under some circumstances, functioned as wives. Not uncommonly, men may marry more than a single wife (polygyny). Extremely rarely, women may marry more than a single husband (polyandry). Children may or may not exhibit genetic linkages with their parents. Indeed, in adolescence and adulthood, both men and women may identify peers with whom they share no immediate genetic linkage as their "sister" or "brother." Fictive kinship may extend between generations to "uncles" or "aunts" or between "fathers" and "sons." By far the most prevalent form of a family consists of a male husband, a female wife, and children of both sexes.

Historically, most human communities organized families into larger units based on the ability to trace relationships between male members, to produce kinship units that we call *patrilineal lineages* and *clans*. A smaller set of communities organized families into larger units based on female affiliations—matrilineal lineages and clans. A tiny set of communities organized themselves into both patrilineal and matrilineal groups of families. Reliably massive runs of oily fish (salmon and trout), sea mammals, game, and plentiful fish and shellfish inshore provided the foundation for relatively large settlements among foragers who lived in the Pacific Northwest from the Eel River in north coast California to Alaska. Residence and affiliations in the north, from the Haida to the Tlingit, emphasized matricentered relationships. In the south, from the Kwakiutl to the Wiyot and Hupa, patricentered descent groups held use rights to specific fishing grounds.

These ways of determining who counts as family did not work elsewhere. They violated the moral admonition that you should allow for maximal rules of affiliation. Foragers, overwhelmingly, did not distinguish ties through mothers and fathers. You were family if you traced relationships through either your mother or your father. Foragers also commonly took a further step to maximize family ties. Friends may bond like sisters or brothers and, so count as family.

Even more important, your ties of family and friendship should extend beyond your immediate residential community. Marriage creates the best ties, so foragers commonly still practice local group exogamy. Rules of exogamy state whom you should not marry. A rule of local group exogamy states that you should find a mate in another camp, which requires mutual visits, significant mobility between and among camps, and long-standing family relationships across wide regions. In lieu of marriage, trading partnerships extend lines of assistance. Some trading partnerships entail quasi-kin relationships, as in the Inupiat practice of "wife lending."

Who may live together? Family. Camps might consist of a single family or many families—albeit rarely more than five to six families. You could join a camp by being born into it, marrying into it, or going to live with your mother, father, son, daughter, brother, sister, father's brother, or mother's sister or—think up some other combination. If you can't find a blood tie to an existing member, you could still move into the camp if you had a "blood" tie to an existing member— based, for example, on a trading partnership.

Synergy and Cultural Designs

We ordinarily characterize the evolution of bipedal humans by the emergence of a gendered division of labor, tools and tool kits of increasing sophistication, and an increasingly fat head and large Encephalization Quotient, and, eventually, language. An ancestor who could talk about what he or she did, when, how, and why, could more readily share his or her knowledge, see things in new ways, and distinguish what works from what doesn't. Sharing knowledge quickens the spread of important innovations and means that your ideas can build on those of others, even if those ideas or ways of doing things originated hundreds or thousands or hundreds of thousands of years earlier. The minds of people who store more information generate both more and more radically different new ways of thinking about the world and acting in it. This informational growth heightens personal awareness that things don't work right and makes finding ways to effectively correct mistakes easier and faster. Significant advantages thus accrued to our ancestors, who, generation after generation, possessed minds that both received and stored increasing amounts of sensory information, processed it in ways that generated increasing numbers of innovations, and effectively shared them increasingly well.

Language acquires these selective advantages, however, only if it can coevolve with other properties of mind. A. F. C Wallace pointed out half a century ago that our life in cooperating groups (he didn't call them *teams* but that, in fact, was what he referred to) gave huge selective advantages to brains that could produce, comprehend, and effectively use innovations such as fire. Individuals break easily; teams don't. Indeed, what counts as a team consists of closely coordinated behavior that makes possible accomplishments that are beyond the capabilities of individuals. Cultures do things when people act on what best corresponds to the moral order for a specific behavioral domain. Cultures accomplish larger goals when the cultures fit well together.

Our ancestors created a set of cultures that fit with one another very well. One culture produced a moral vision that told its participants how to identify and respond resiliently to the uncertainties and dangers of the world. Another produced a moral vision that told its participants how to create teams based on mutual dependencies across large distances and many groups—dependencies not enforced by individuals but that individuals negotiated with one another. The last produced a moral vision that told its participants how to do all this with family members, the most reliable sources of help. Together—indeed, only together—these cultures produced a flourishing, not merely surviving, human population. They flourished in the face of the last major glacial period. They flourished in the face of the Toba supereruption that some 74,000 years ago reduced the number of humans on the planet to 3,000–10,000. Our ancestors, few as they were, appear to have left Africa around 70,000 years ago. Within 50,000 years over course of what we now call the Late Paleolithic, we covered the planet. We lived in the Arctic, the desert, and the rainforest, on the seashore and at 10,000 feet.

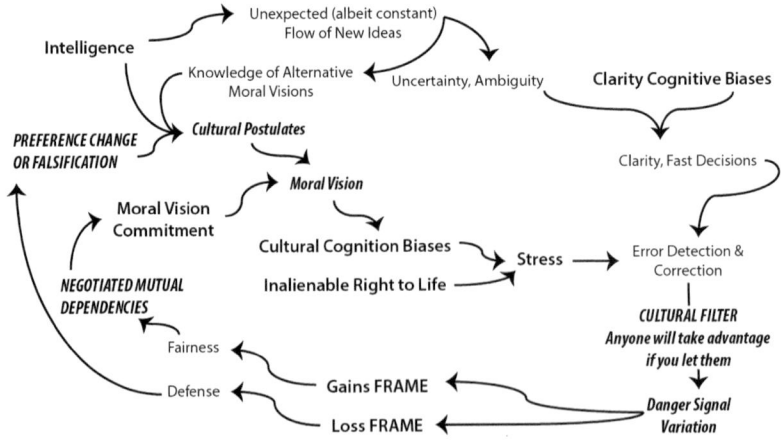

Figure 4.1

We eventually thrived with a mind characterized by the coevolution of intelligence and language with properties that enabled us to:

- make decisions quickly,
- detect and winnow out errors,
- see and then enforce compliance with the moral vision of specific activity domains that differentiate teams from aggregations, and
- detect and respond to threats to us as individuals.

Part II of *Our Story* describes these mechanisms and how they work.

Part II

On the Properties of Mind that Produce Agency

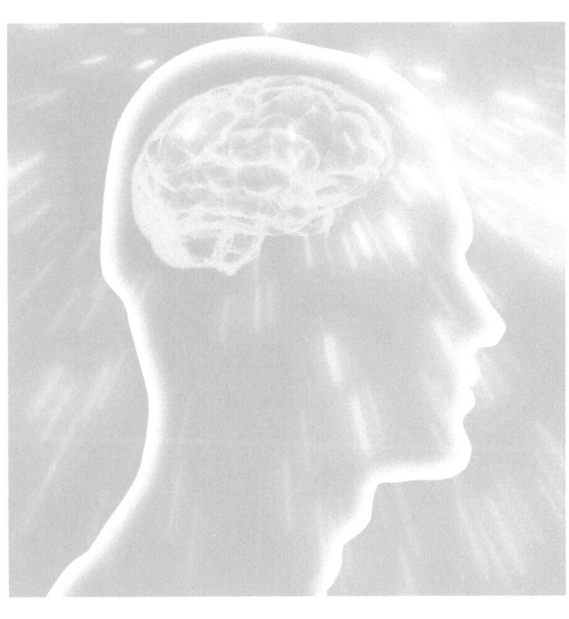

Chapter 5

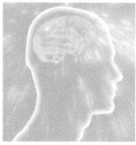

Coercive Force Yields Morally Ordered Behavior

Cultural designs originate in our imaginations, as we discussed in Chapter 1. Imagining properties of the world in which we live allows us to find new ways to do things when old ways prove ineffective, if not dangerous. One set of imaginative outputs creates the things of our world. Another set creates postulates about specific behavioral domains that imply a specific moral vision for that domain.

Honor Cultures

For example, one culture widespread in the southern portion of the United States speculates that the world is a dangerous place, that family is most important, that women in the family are in the most danger, so men in the family should protect them. You learn from boyhood that you should take care of your mother and protect your sisters. That, in fact, is your primary job, which after you are married applies also to your wife. You also learn that negotiating mutual dependences with a wide network of friends (who may include employees, employers, and coworkers) counts as the best way to do your job well. These mutual dependencies, very much like those created among foragers, rest on the agreement of all involved that the network members remain loyal to one another. You thus also learn from boyhood that you should consistently acknowledge mistakes and seek to rectify them, treat everyone with kindness and respect, remain loyal to both family and friends and, in a word, live *honorably*.

As David Fischer pointed out in his 1989 book *Albion's Seed*, the Cavaliers who settled Virginia and the adjacent Chesapeake Bay tidewater areas gave America a strain of individualism and independence jealous of its privileges and hostile to local authority, founded on the cultural norm of personal integrity and kindness to others.

Scots-English borderers who settled the American frontier shortly afterward gave America a strain of distrust of institutionalized authorities, reliance on trust based on personal knowledge of specific people, individualism highly sensitive to threats to personal well-being, and fast, aggressive responses to those threats with the most effective weapons available. Both Cavalier and Scots-English borderer traditions and more went into the creation of the U.S. Constitution. Both also produced the South's honor culture.

What happens if you change the postulates? You create another honor culture but one with a moral vision so different that, if you grew up in the honor culture of the South, it shocks your soul.

Let's keep the assumptions that the world is a dangerous place and that family is most important. Let's assume, by contrast, *not* that women in the family are in the most danger *but* that women's sexuality poses the most danger to families. That small change shifts the moral vision from one in which men in the family should protect the women to one in which men must control the sexuality of their female family members to protect the family. Among the most dishonorable acts that women can commit are entering into marriage having lost their virginity, exhibiting sexual interest in anyone not approved by the men of the family, and adultery. In fact, these are among the most egregious acts anyone may undertake and qualify for the most egregious sanctions. In the South's honor culture, men would (and have) died to keep their women safe. In the alternative honor culture, widely spread over, most notably, the Middle East and South Asia, fathers/sons/brothers readily bury their "dishonorable" wives and daughters up to their shoulders so they may be stoned to death efficiently; fathers/sons/brothers readily behead their mother or sister or niece.

In his 2009 (revised) book *On Killing*, Lt. Col. Dave Grossman assembles a strong argument that humans find it extraordinarily hard to kill each other and do so only under specific circumstances. The circumstances? A culture that says that is the right thing to do and backs up the moral assertion with significant consequences. The importance of kinship ties means that it must be dramatically more difficult to kill a person with whom you share a large quantity of your own genes. Hbd chick (http://hbdchick.wordpress.com/) makes a compelling argument that honor killings count as an important example of inclusive fitness, because "the altruistic individual's genes that are sacrificed on behalf of copies of his genes in other individuals are *other* copies of his genes in *other* individuals." But this act becomes biologically altruistic only because, in this form of an honor culture, surviving children may not be able to marry.

The power of a culture to enforce its moral vision, as do the postulates on which a culture rests, comes from our minds. In *The Origin of Cultures* (2009) I pointed out that cultures exhibit the properties of a thing, because recurrent behavior constitutes an environment in which we carry out daily activities and that elicits cognitive, emotional, and behavioral responses. Certain forms of recurrent, patterned behaviors (for example,, those that produce childhood traumatic stress) may induce specific, lifelong changes in how our minds work and in the behavioral trajectory of our lives. In 2009 I focused on how our mind allows us to learn some things and not others. Here I broaden that discussion to identify evolved mechanisms that our minds use to transform cultural postulates and moral visions into effective teams.

We Call Them Cognitive Biases

Imagine the existential questions our ancestors faced:
- Why can't we find game this season?
- Is it time to move?
- What's best—to share with this person or kill him/her?

Because our minds come up with fanciful stories, one effect of constant innovation—even when it allows resilient responses to unexpected changes in our environment — consists of error, ambiguity, and uncertainty. The things we've come to call "cognitive biases" clear up ambiguities and uncertainties so we can make decisions quickly, detect and winnow out egregious errors, and see and enforce compliance with the moral vision of specific activity domains that differentiates teams from aggregations,.

One Set Reduces Our Uncertainties

Deer-in-the-headlights dithering sets you up for failure, of course. "Learned helplessness" may count as the most dramatic form of inaction. Mammals, including humans, learn helplessness when exposed to uncontrollable traumatic stress. The most plausible mechanism posits that when you are subject to traumatic stress that your behavior cannot affect, a drop in norepinephrine means that your mind cannot clearly see any solutions to problems. The word "panic" nicely captures the phenomenon. Subsequent increases in norepinephrine production "unlearn" the mind from helplessness.

Because panic inhibits our ability to delay death, eat reliably, and reproduce, selection would very strongly favor people whose minds evolved unconscious cognitive biases to transform ambiguity into predictable, reliable findings. Think of "closure" for example. Gestalt psychologists observed early in the 20th century that we see things as whole entities even when (as, probably, nearly all the time) significant parts are missing. Our minds seek a different form of closure when we experience traumatic experiences like the death of a child or parent or rejection by a lover. *Cognitive dissonance* and *dissonance reduction* mechanisms, likewise, yield clarity. Our minds respond to conflicts between ideas or ideas and behavior once they come into consciousness (dissonance) by resolving the conflict (dissonance reduction). If your fiancée doesn't show up at the wedding, she wasn't right for you anyway. If you can't think of how to reach those grapes, they must be sour (h/t Aesop). Notoriously, political conservatives were, before the mugging, bleeding heart liberals who assume that all people are naturally good. Anne Frank maintained that position—read her *The Diary of a Young Girl* (h/t

Bookworm)—even while she, with family and friends, went into hiding to avoid capture and shipment to a death camp. Her diary ends August 1, 1944, three days before betrayal led to shipment first to Auschwitz and later to Bergen-Belsen. We don't know if she changed her mind before she died. Hard to understand how she couldn't have, given the intense cognitive dissonance produced by life in the camps.

But maybe she didn't. Cognitive dissonance counts as only one of many cognitive mechanisms that transform confusion into clarity. Others include the ostrich effect, the confirmatory bias, and related mental mechanisms. These processes explain, for example, why, as Ed Green pointed out in the 2011 book *Broken Promises*, the global AIDS establishment blinded themselves to the effectiveness of ABC (Abstain, Be faithful, use Condoms) intervention cultures and thus helped kill millions of Africans. They also explain why leaders in science dismissed out of hand Barbara McClintock's evidence for jumping genes, Stanley Prusiner's evidence for a new infectious agent he called *prions*, and Dan Schechtman's evidence for quasicrystals—all of which led to Nobel Prizes. Our minds don't easily tell us that we messed up. Which explains why we recognize the wisdom in comments like Napoleon Bonaparte's observation: "Never interrupt your enemy when he is making a mistake."

Our imaginations have been captured by egregious examples, like these, of how cognitive biases produce bad choices. We should refocus. Evolved mechanisms come into being because they contribute to an organism's ability to avoid predation and exploitation, eat, and reproduce. Thus, it makes no sense to characterize something as maladaptive unless it contributes to relative reproductive failure either directly or through impaired abilities to avoid predation and exploitation or to obtain access to resources. Evolved mechanisms contribute to an organism's ability to avoid predation/ex-

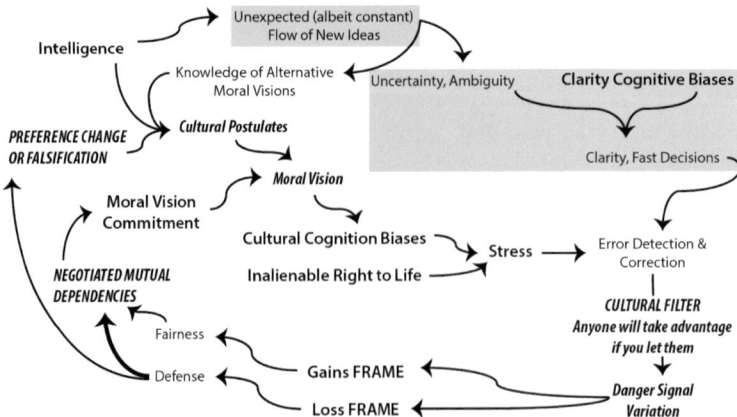

Figure 5.1

ploitation, eat, and reproduce when they respond sensitively to environmental changes. Yes, biases may lead us to faulty conclusions. But not always and probably only rarely.

For example, *wishful thinking* counts as a form of cognitive bias particularly divorced from reality, and one that could have no adaptive value whatsoever. Not so. Recent research spearheaded by Richard Sosis closely examined a form of wishful thinking exhibited by Israeli women subject to Katyusha rocket attacks during the 2006 Lebanon war—recitation of Psalms. Sosis was following up a suggestion made by Bronislaw Malinowski in his 1935 book *Coral Gardens and Their Magic* that people create magical rituals when faced with important forms of uncertainty. Since we can't consciously do this, it would be more accurate to say that people's *minds* create magical rituals when faced with uncertainty (today, we'd restrict this claim to the uncontrollable evolutionarily significant trauma that could induce learned helplessness). In any event, it turns out that Malinowski was right. Psalm recitation calmed its participants in the face of uncontrollable uncertainty of loss and death from rocket attacks. Psalm recitation, like other ritual expressions, probably does so because it induces an increase in norepinephrine production that, in the face or otherwise panic-inducing experiences, allows its participants to see more clearly and make better choices.

Recent findings by Friese and Wänke published in the *Journal of Experimental Social Psychology* (http://dx.doi.org/10.1016/j.jesp.2013.11.006) show that prayer—talking to G-d—gives people strength. Believers, of course, already know this from personal experience.

The nature of our mind precludes errorless choices. What counts is the ability to identify errors quickly and alter choices in ways that may produce better consequences. Cognitive biases that force us to recreate familiar environments not only clarify our choices, they minimize error. Which explains why Americans overseas create little American communities that re-create, to the extent possible, the world from which they came. These include swimming pools and swimming lessons, tennis courts and tennis lessons, and American schools built so that, inside, you can't tell if you're in Moline, Illinois, or Redding, California, or Accra, Ghana. The cultural patterns that our Foreign Service officers bring with them come predominantly from white, upper- to upper-middle class, Anglo-Saxon, Protestant America. Which explains why you can still see much Russian influence in Harbin, China, some Portuguese influence in Macau, British influence in Hong Kong and America, and West African influences in Brazil, the West Indies, and the U.S. South.

A Second Set Detects Errors and Highlights Opportunities

Without a mechanism to differentiate the things of our imagination with empirical content from mistakes, which don't, we'd be lost, and intelligent minds could not exist. The solution? Emotionally weighted memories called *heuristic*s. Scholars have labeled many cognitive biases as one or another kind of heuristic. Most so-called heuristics function,

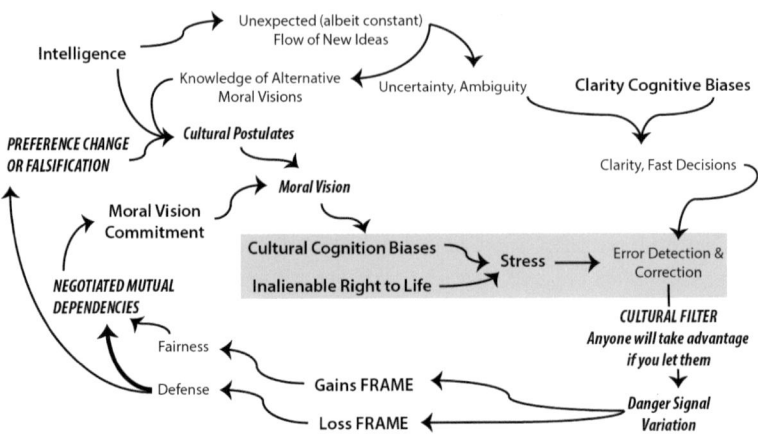

Figure 5.2

like *wishful thinking* and *closure*, as means to achieve clarity quickly. Emotionally laden memories, however, distinguish dangers from opportunities.

When you think about it, we'd be sorely pressed to explain how we—well, how any life form— could exist without a mechanism sensitive to the consequences of our choices. Moreover, only some properties of our choices have any bearing on our well-being. The change a specific consequence produces in the likelihood that an organism will avoid death, eat well reliably, and thus optimize its reproductive success surely counts as the most important. Because you can't get to tomorrow unless you make it through today, selection necessarily gives priority to short-run success. This means that our minds had to evolve a means to differentiate good from bad consequences, the immediacy with which they happen, and the certainty of experiencing a specific consequence, good or bad.

We call the mechanism that assigns emotional weights to experiences *stress*. Stress as many people conceive of it, as a homeostatic response to environmental demands— or our interpretation of environmental stimuli that tax or exceed the adaptive capacity of an organism—completely misses its importance. Stress also cements these emotionally weighted experiences in our long-term memory. During stress, attention increases and thus becomes more focused, even in the absence of awareness. Stress thus enhances cognitive abilities to identify opportunities or threats, to respond to an opportunity or threat optimally, and to store pertinent declarative and habitual memories. Working memory may suffer deficits. But declarative and habitual memory tend to be encoded particularly effectively. Effective memory encoding enhances our ability to successfully anticipate and avoid, respond to, or take advantage of equivalent future opportunities or threats. We call the cognition bias outcome *heuristics* because these memories quickly surface and use our experience to powerfully shape our responses to environmental variation in threats and opportunities.

Stress responses exhibit their highest intensity when the threat or opportunity is great relative to any alternative, bears on one's ability to avoid predation or exploitation, requires an immediate response, and when the outcome is highly uncertain. Increasing response times yield corresponding greater prefrontal cortex control of behavior and more measured responses. With long response times, the presence of competing stressors or opportunities redirects stress and may account for Parkinson's Law—our propensity to allow tasks to fill the time we have to complete them.

No Choice, or Free to Choose?

By assigning emotional weights to stressors and supports, stress induces choices that correspond with the difference in weights. Increasing weight differences should correspond with increasing probabilities that people choose the alternative with the greatest weight. We experience freedom of choice when all members of a set of alternatives bear equal weights. In these circumstances, the probability of choosing any one alternative should equal the probability of choosing any other alternative. Alternatives that cannot be differentiated in cost are selectively neutral. Neither alternative may reduce or improve our well-being, or both (or all) alternatives may reduce or improve our well-being by equal amounts. To be clear, probably you experience only trivial consequence differences among breakfast choices of a bowl of cereal, eggs and bacon, coffee and donut, or nothing. Similarly, you experience only trivial consequence differences among running for the doorway, ducking under a desk, attempting to hide in a corner, or climbing out the window if you find yourself caught in room with a maniac shooter. People are free to choose among alternatives like these on highly personal and even whimsical grounds. Indeed, genuine "freedom of choice" exists only when you can choose among selectively neutral alternatives. Panic may ensue when we face two choices that kill us. But the probability of choice still should approximate 50/50.

These emotional weights, which in consciousness we rationalize as costs and benefits, determine the likelihood that you, or I, or any specific person, will choose one alternative rather than the other. This feature of our minds thus constitutes a selective mechanism responsible for the production of new or the maintenance or change of preexisting patterns of behavior. We differentiate alternatives by their costs relative to their potential benefits. The presence and intensity of selective pressures thus may be measured as cost differentials.

Cost differences between alternatives constrain your freedom to choose, and agency doesn't exist when you have no choice. Intense selection pressure thus creates behavioral uniformity. Little or no selection pressure makes for behavioral diversity. For a simple example, look around you at how people dress. Seasonal climatic change means a shift in the consequences of dressing lightly or heavily, so you rarely see someone wearing shorts in a New England winter or someone wearing a down parka in the summer heat and humidity of South Florida. It makes little difference, however, whether you wear yellow or red or blue. The absence of difference produces a lot of diversity in how people dress lightly or heavily. Employment cultures, party cultures, and some school cultures often come with more significant consequences for departures from dress norms. Offices, parties, and parochial schools generally exhibit relative uniformity in dress. The absence of consequences for dress variations in public school cultures, by contrast, creates much dress variation. Because not wearing clothes brings with it significant consequences everywhere outside of nudist camps, however, everyone wears clothes.

A Third Set Makes Us Pay Special Attention to People!

> He who listens to a life-giving rebuke will be at home among the wise. He who ignores discipline despises himself, but whoever heeds correction gains understanding. (Proverbs 15: 31–32)

The power of a consequence—whether it comes in the form of

- nasty looks and scolding,
- public rebukes and scolding,
- fines,
- slit ears or tongues,
- a cut off hand or arm or leg, or
- death by decapitation, stoning, firing squad, or needle—

comes from your imagination. Not—I repeat—*not* from the material properties of the consequence. Death may transform you from an ordinary person to a hero. Nasty looks and hurtful words may kill you.

To reiterate—we give the things of our world meaning, because we must (well, our Interpreter must) speculate about its nature. Those speculations imply a moral vision shared by the community in which we grow up. All the clarity in the world about which choice may kill you or improve your life won't help a person who pays no attention to the most immediate sources of life and death—the people with whom they live. Our minds, consequently, contain a large number of cognitive biases that, without our volition, force us to pay close attention to people and how they respond to us.

Our minds automatically look for information that tells the difference between friend and foe. Our minds notice variations in skill and performance competences. We praise excellence and criticize incompetence. We pay particular attention to how people evaluate us. Praise from others makes us feel good. Star quarterbacks given the highest salary ever handed out by an NFL team now feels "respected." Criticism, by contrast, produces anxiety and anger. Our brain employs cognitive biases, consequently, that make choices in ways to avoid criticism and invite praise—like the *hindsight bias* (we knew it all along), the *self-serving bias* (which leads us to attribute good things to ourselves whether warranted by actual achievements or not), the *Hawthorne effect* (worker productivity increases in the presence of observers), and the *Dunning-Kruger effect* (incompetents fail to recognize their own incompetence—which explains why we find it so difficult to acknowledge error).

We feel safest in familiar circumstances, and our minds automatically shift our behavior in ways that make us more similar to the people we interact with. The latter, called the *chameleon effect,* applies to husbands and wives who grow more similar in habits and speech forms, as well as to extensive culture regions—Polynesia and Micronesia in the Pacific, for example, or the Great Basin and California in the American West—which invariably exhibit cultural clines as one culture area turns slowly into the other. The chameleon effect reflects the frequency and intensity of social interaction and, thus, interaction barriers that create distance in time, space, or behavior. We see the chameleon effect in action when both Puerto Rican and Connecticut Yankee parents show no differences in how they think about parent-teacher relationships and in the dialect chains over large distances that make it impossible to say precisely where in Europe the Spanish language ends and the French language begins or in West Africa where the Grebo language ends and the Khran language begins. Because the chameleon effect, like other cognitive biases, operates without our volition, distinctive cultural communities— whether Chinatown, Little Saigon, or Muslim enclaves across Europe—show evidence of barriers to its operation.

Human relationships exhibit dynamics that vary with the relative power of the actors. Max Weber pointed out in 1922 that *power* is the ability to influence or to control the behavior and beliefs of others even without their consent. Power comes from the capacity of one agent to inflict evolutionarily significant consequences on another. The capacity to inflict these consequences accrues to any given agent to the extent to which it serves as gatekeeper for access to means of survival and resource access for clients. Power grows with the importance of the resources involved and the number of clients. Cultures—assumptions we share with others and the moral vision they produce count as gatekeepers for access to our means of survival and to resources. The cultural agreement counts as the agent, and all members of the cultures count as clients. Cultures do things when behavior corresponds with the moral vision. You as an individual get the benefits. But only if you go along. Cognitive biases like *in-group bias*, the *bandwagon effect*, *groupthink*, *stereotyping*, *essentialism*, and *the status quo bias* give us the tools to do just that. Our culture thus tells us to whom to grant authority. The *halo effect* extends that authority far beyond a specific person's skills and abilities.

Cognitive Coercion Yields Success

The people who make up our cultural communities count as our most important source of assistance, because our cultures determine what we can or cannot do. They made it possible to go from a population of 3,000–10,000 on the entire planet to more than

7 billion people today. They tell how to be Gay, make it through Law School, make a profit selling food or sex, avoid bad teeth, and make a bundle handing out subprime loans that you didn't want to deal with but could resell at a big profit to your friends in government. It's why, as of 2014, the four of the wealthiest counties in the United States, with 6-figure median incomes, cluster around Washington, DC.

Cultures act like agents because they dictate the options and choices from which cultural participants may choose—what's there, who's there, and what participants should or should not do. Our cultures tell us what counts as fair and just—that's implicit in the moral vision produced by shared postulates about the nature of a behavioral domain. The existence of culturally defined fair and just behavior implies that violations must be reliably detected (h/t Leda Cosmides and John Tooby and colleagues) and punished (h/t Joseph Henrich and colleagues). Just as cognitive biases lead us to identify and punish moral vision violations, other cognitive biases force us to pay attention to our cultural community and give weight to corrective signals from cultural authorities. These include the spanking, cuffing, and equivalent physical punishments that parents may inflict on their children, the periodic hurtful words that all individuals inflict occasionally on others, and most of the physical and emotional violence in which children and adolescents commonly engage as they compete for status and establish social boundaries.

These constraints mean that individuals cannot accomplish anything on their own. Individual accomplishments rest on participation in a culture in which the activities of one person coordinate with those of others. Individuals can't even kill people effectively to defend themselves, particularly if in dying they accomplish an important cultural goal. Because a culture makes it so easy to go with the flowing consensus and so hard to buck that tide, a culture will take you to *its* destination whether you want to or not. As Wes Moore points out in his *The Other Wes Moore* (2011), we respond to the expectations (aka cultural norms) of our fellow cultural participants. Two Wes Moores, growing up blocks away from one another, fatherless, hanging out with gangs, involved with drugs, trouble with the police. A small difference in cultural postulates took one Wes Moore to prison and the other to a Rhodes Scholarship.

The same people who make up our cultural communities thus count simultaneously as our most dangerous threat. The group speculations we call cultural assumptions and the group findings about the moral vision these assumptions yield are as prone to error as the individual minds from which they came.

Chapter 6

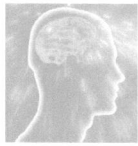

Cognitive Coercion May Kill You Before You Get Anywhere

Mass suicides count as perhaps the most dramatic example. Whether at Masada in 73 A.D., the self-destruction of civilians following the fall of Saipan in World War II, or the Jonestown suicides in Guyana, mass suicides express commitment to a shared moral vision that a community should deny the ability to impose on its members the cultural norms of an enemy.

Terrorist attacks rationalized by a distinctive set of cultural norms constitute the most dramatic forms of violence in the contemporary world. Between the mid-20th century and the first years of the 21st century, terrorist incidents skyrocketed from one to two incidents per year to three per day. Israelis alone have experienced nearly 1,000 terror attacks since the signing of the Oslo agreement in 1993, which was intended to establish nonviolent relations between Israel and Palestine. But terrorist attacks have also killed Russians, Americans, British, Danes, Canadians, Saudis, Germans, French, Egyptians, Jordanians, Indians, Australians, Japanese, Filipinos, Indonesians, Pakistanis, Iraqis, Swiss, and Afghanis. Terrorists left Dutch filmmaker Theo van Gogh dead on the sidewalk with a knife in his chest and the editor of a Sudanese newspaper, Mohammed Taha, without a head. Terrorist threats drove Hirsi Ali, a member of the Dutch parliament, to flee to the United States and Seyran Ates, a German women's rights lawyer who won the Berlin Women's Prize in 2004 and a Civil Courage Prize in 2005, to close her law practice.

The norms? Democracies should be destroyed; and all individuals guilty of apostasy, Muslim or non-Muslim, should be killed.

The cultural postulates, according to Sayyid Qutb (1964)?

- Allah constitutes the highest authority for human affairs;

- Shari'a, based primarily on the word of Allah (the Qur'an) and the practices of the Prophet Muhammad, constitute the ultimate law for all humans;
- apostasy consists of any rejection of the first two principles and constitutes a crime punishable by death;
- Muslims who reject the first two principles, any non-Muslim who rejects Islam by failing to convert, and democracies, because they assume that the people who are governed constitute the ultimate authority for human affairs, count as examples of apostasy.

The frequency of these kinds of terrorist incidents, however, pales in comparison to another form of violence that terrorizes its recipient, violence against women. Violence to women, whether rationalized with religious postulates or not, always rests on imagined inherent differences and inequalities between men and women that yield a moral vision that requires violence to punish norm violations by women. Data collected in the United States through the National Violence Against Women Survey indicate that 5.3 million terrorist incidents of this kind occur to women each year. These result in nearly 2 million injuries, 8 million days of lost paid work, and around 5.6 million days of lost household work. Because the effects of such violence accumulate, the severity and breadth of sequelae are especially problematic. The direct effects of violence include scratches, bruises, welts, lacerations, knife wounds, broken bones, head injuries, sore muscles, internal injuries, broken teeth, burns, bullet wounds, and death. Sequelae of violence include everything from an elevated risk of STDs/HIV, PID, and cervical cancer through depression and PTSD through suicide attempts, homicide by the victim, and later homicide of an initial survivor. Significant trauma from intimate partner violence extends to men as well as women. Within the United States, violence thus entails huge social and economic costs. The CDC has estimated the annual costs of intimate partner violence against women in the United States at $5.8 billion. Violence to children, however, accompanies violence to women. Violence to children, whether structural or direct, produces violence in the next generation. The costs of the assaults, robberies, and murder by adults who were abused as children add another $8.6 billion, which makes the annual cost of violence in the United States exceed the budgets of the Department of the Interior, Labor, Commerce, or the Treasury and approximate the budget for the Department of Justice (CDC 2003).

Among equals, we prize comity. Sometimes our wish for comity produces determined attempts to believe in the face of dramatic evidence of betrayal. The outcomes may count as trivial, as when faith in specific authorities damages us. The outcomes may count as significant, as when, until December 6, 2009, the day she disappeared, Susan Powell documented in her diary faith in an authoritative idea—repairing her marriage to an increasingly controlling and violent man, in the presence of a father-in-law who sought uncomfortable levels of intimacy—despite fear for her life.

Figure 6.1

MISSING PERSON
SUSAN POWELL

Mising From:
West Valley City, Utah
Date Missing:
12/07/2009
Age: 28 Years Old
Sex: Female
Height: 5 feet 4 Inches
Weight: 130 pounds
Hair: Brown, Long
Eyes: Blue

Susan Powell was last seen at her home in West Valley City, Utah on Sunday night, December 6, 2009. Susan was reported missing on Monday, December 7th. It is unknown if she went on foot or by vehicle. It is also not known if she went on her own or with anyone. Anyone with information, or if you have seen Susan is asked to please contact the police.

West Valley Police Department
801-840-4000

Innocent and well-meaning attempts to support friends and family may kill just as certainly. Sometimes our wish for comity produces what in 1974 Jerry Harvey called The Abilene Paradox:

> On a hot afternoon visiting in Coleman, Texas, the family is comfortably playing dominoes on a porch, until the father-in-law suggests that they take a trip to Abilene [53 miles north] for dinner. The wife says, "Sounds like a great idea." The husband, despite having reservations because the drive is long and hot, thinks that his preferences must be out-of-step with the group and says, "Sounds good to me. I just hope your mother wants to go." The mother-in-law then says, "Of course I want to go. I haven't been to Abilene in a long time."
>
> The drive is hot, dusty, and long. When they arrive at the cafeteria, the food is as bad as the drive. They arrive back home four hours later, exhausted.
>
> One of them dishonestly says, "It was a great trip, wasn't it?" The

mother-in-law says that, actually, she would rather have stayed home but went along since the other three were so enthusiastic. The husband says, "I wasn't delighted to be doing what we were doing. I only went to satisfy the rest of you." The wife says, "I just went along to keep you happy. I would have had to be crazy to want to go out in the heat like that." The father-in-law then says that he suggested it only because he thought the others might be bored.

The group sits back, perplexed that they together decided to take a trip that none of them wanted. They each would have preferred to sit comfortably but did not admit to it when they still had time to enjoy the afternoon.

Sometimes, however, we go along wishing well for all, and die. One Abilene Paradox killed all but two of a Russian-American research team. It would have killed the remaining two people had one not been in Kamchatka and had the other "gone it alone" on the grounds that a trip to a research site, Sireniki, was too dangerous. The story that eventually came out was one of a series of grossly irresponsible decisions, each one of which cut the team members' envelope of safety, until none was left. In simple terms, they did not respect the water. Each one of the team had spent his entire professional career working in the North, where there's little enough room for errors. They knew that a major cause of death was trauma, and the biggest chunk of this, in Russia, was boats that went to sea and did not return. Yet they left Sireniki with a drunk boat master and overloaded the boat with three additional passengers. They made it about two-thirds of the way to Provideniya (which would have been around 6 P.M. the night they were returning), just around the corner of the bay—we know, because a skin boat heading from Provideniya to Sireniki saw them, came up beside them, pointed out that they were overloaded, and offered to take the three additional passengers back to Provideniya before they continued on to Sireniki. They refused.

Many Orcas and California Grey Whales had been seen in the vicinity in recent weeks, and the boat that found the "broken boat" had spotted an immature Grey. Greys are known to be territorial in this area, aggressive, not placid as they apparently are where they mate, off Baja California. I suspect they spotted a whale. One team member, R, not thinking things through as usual, wanted to get closer. A Russian team member, S_r, shaving the edge as usual, agreed. S_r's American counterpart, S_a, would have been concerned but would have agreed to support S_r. B, who would have been justifiably scared, would not want to embarrass S_a. They got too close. Maybe an Orca got curious. Maybe a mother Grey became aggressive. The drunk boat master couldn't react fast enough; the additional passengers would have made the boat even more awkward to handle in an emergency.

"Going along" means that we count as an error a choice that elicits criticism, and we seek to change in ways that avoid criticism even if they do not receive praise. Sometimes we're unsuccessful. Introspection reveals consistently how these memories of past errors shape some of our most fundamental life choices. It might mean something as simple as choosing to enroll at a local state university because, having grown up in poverty, you are terrified about going into debt. Or, because you experienced a variety of physical, sexual, and emotional traumas as a child, your brain produces intense needs for affection at the same time that you feel intensely angry and scared, emotions that then propel you into and out of relationships and much self-medication.

You have to "go it alone" sometimes. If you can't find a way to escape, the simplest, most innocent-sounding words—when hurled by cultural authorities—will kill you.

Who Cares if Sticks and Stones May Break Your Bones When Words Can Kill You?

Words like "you." They kill slowly, insidiously, but they kill as surely as a bullet. The "cause of death" may be a drug overdose, HIV/AIDS, cirrhosis of the liver, cervical cancer, lung cancer, suicide, or heart disease. But the real killer was the word "you," heard too often as a child, in hurtful comments made by people with cultural authority—parents talking to their children, teachers talking to students, star athletes talking to nerds.

And long before they kill, words like "you" maim. During a child's school years, such words lead to depression and so to poor school performance, aggressive behavior, and alienation from peers. During school and afterward, they make it nearly impossible to create fulfilling social relationships. Tobacco, alcohol, and illicit drugs often substitute. Girls and boys move from one sexual partner to another and acquire and pass along sexually transmitted diseases. Girls get pregnant and bear children long before they can function effectively as a parent. Self-medicating girls, who may simultaneously be HIV-positive, give birth to children with their own drug dependencies, HIV-positive diagnoses, and neurological damage. Research in Antigua in 1988 and 1989 (Handwerker 2003), for example, produced a set of empirical models that allow us to express concretely the contrasting effects on adolescent girls of violent and predatory (that is, exploitative) or affectionate and supportive (that is, nonexploitative) childhood environments. Both groups initiated sexual activity at age 12. Exploited Antiguan adolescents invested in childbearing far more than women who grew up in exploitation-free homes. Girls who grew up in exploitation-free homes acquired 4 different sexual partners, achieved acceptable passes on secondary school final examinations, and averaged about 1 child by age 20. In contrast, girls who experienced intense exploitation (including non-incestuous sexual predation at age 12), acquired 7 different partners by age 20, averaged only 6 to 10 years of schooling, and bore 2 children by age 20.

Once children subject to trauma in childhood become parents, ongoing depression commonly impairs their ability to pay appropriate attention to their children or to remain calm when dealing with the stresses that parenting inevitably brings. Their fear of closeness and dependence on another makes it nearly impossible to maintain two-parent families. And those who don't die early of overt suicide, drug overdoses, or the violence that surrounds the use of illicit drugs and tend to experience a variety of physical impairments including chronic and incapacitating pain, fatigue, and headaches. And they die early of cancer and cardiovascular disease.

Children's brains continue to grow and develop through adolescence. Hurtful words and looks yield the effects just described by changing how the brain develops and thus how it works in adulthood. The effects of stress coming from events like moving to a new school, or even the death of a parent, pale in comparison to the effects of stress coming to us in the form of words that hurt. A Russian-American study of Social Transition in the North, headed by Alexander Pika and Steve McNabb, for example, found that childhood violence experiences exhibit clear and strong relationships with current symptoms of depression, regardless of the time since exposure—for up to 83 years (Handwerker 1999).

In the 1990s I was privileged to work on this project alongside Bill Richards, a psychiatrist with long experience working in the Indian Health Service in Alaska. Bill described a clinical case of a suicide attempter that, too commonly, he encountered in Alaskan native communities:

> A younger sister was mentally retarded, probably from fetal alcohol syndrome, and the next oldest sister was marginally retarded, probably from fetal alcohol effects. The boy's father had died when he was young from an alcohol-related accident. The boy had been sodomized repeatedly by an older brother while growing up. He describes himself now, at age 28, as feeling like a "life-time of failure," who was "born sick." He has trouble concentrating and appears unable to maintain direction in occupational and subsistence activities. He appears to have severe difficulty in areas of independent living skills, impulse control, and judgment and has recently been involving himself in sexually abusing a young child. He abuses alcohol and does not comply well with treatment programs. The clinicians conclude that "lacking supervision and external direction, he is socially maladaptive." He creates situations, in a somewhat manipulative way, where he needs to be helped, getting quite angry at times, or suicidal, with many expectations that nonnative agency workers or his family members look after his basic needs and provide him financial and other help. At times, he presents his problems as spiritual ones, with talk about being possessed by devils, religious persecution, etc. and at times has been unsuccessfully treated by the psychiatric system. He refuses to comply with medical treatment, and he has a gun with which at times he threatens to shoot himself or others. One gets a feeling from him best described as "impotent rage." (pers. comm.)

This case included no information about hurtful words, but our analyses revealed that hurtful words hurled by parental and generational authorities at their children produced the symptoms described earlier, but they did not produce suicide. Native children died from suicide in frightening numbers owing to hurtful words hurled by new cultural authorities.

We thus discovered, by contrast, that violence directed at natives by nonnatives produced dramatically different effects. Bill pointed out that, historically, indigenous culture in Alaska and the Russian Far East exhibited many elements that could be summarized as "respect"—for nature, for Elders, for children, for animals (see Part I, for example). The culture that had evolved for several thousand years among people living in Arctic communities entailed relatively clear understandings bearing on life and living, of what was right and wrong, and of personal and social responsibilities and obligations and the consequences of behavior that ran counter to community understandings. The former moral vision was replaced with a new one based on laws, rights, and entitlements. And in Alaska, what began in the 1950s and 1960s as a civil and human rights movement in an era of "rights" appears 20–30 years later to have evolved into an era of "entitlement." From being "one with the land," for example, we are now in an era of "land claims," "property rights," and advocacy. There is more anger and ethnic tension in Northern communities and, at the same time, a sense of hostile dependency on government programs. Extended family support and ceremonial activities associated with child-rearing are being replaced with welfare workers, child protection teams, family courts, and ombudsmen. These changes come with associated feelings of being cut off, alienated, blocked, trapped, and hopeless, with limited access to opportunities or power to control resources. What had existed as a clear sense of personal and social responsibilities and consequences for misbehavior now appears as moral ambiguity that makes itself apparent in a lack of integration within communities, families, and individuals.

Alaskan natives thus became subject to frightening and uncontrollable uncertainties with structural discontinuity in the regional economy that produced new resources (education and jobs in a newly constructed resource extraction economy) and radical changes in the cost structure of resource access. Nonnatives poured into Alaska and the Russian Far East and assumed primary control over the new resources. Relations between natives and nonnatives changed dramatically, if only because the huge influx of nonnatives soon made it impossible for natives to avoid intimate and almost daily and all too often demeaning and controlling contact with nonnatives. Over the course of the 1950s and 1960s, village populations declined as people moved to the permanent settlements, which grew into hub towns. Gender relations changed dramatically, too, as they have elsewhere in the world. Women more than men took advantage of educational opportunities that provided access to jobs and cash incomes. Moreover, women alone experienced the opportunity to affiliate themselves with the growing population of nonnative men who filled the newly created means of subsistence. In our total sample— collected in hub towns and affiliated villages in Chukotka and Kamchatka in the Russian Far East and in the Aleutians and the NANA region of Alaska—of 720 men and women, for example, 73% of the nonnative study participants affiliated with nonnative partners, and there exists no difference between men and women. Likewise, 73% of the native study participants affiliated with native partners. But whereas 84% of native men affiliated with native partners, only 69% of native women affiliated with native partners. Read in the other direction, whereas 16% of native men affiliated with nonnative partners, nearly twice the proportion of native women (31%) affiliated with nonnative partners. Just as native men in both Alaska and the Russian Far East generally found themselves at a competitive disadvantage relative to nonnative men for good jobs, they also found themselves at a competitive disadvantage for the relatively small supply of partners, whether native or nonnative. Native men thus found themselves having to select partners from a pool that included many women not acceptable to nonnatives.

Figure 6.2 shows historical variation in the proportion of native children subject to emotional violence by nonnative authorities in Alaska and the Russian Far East. These time series in this figure were constructed from data elicited from study participants on childhood violence reports, which I describe in my methods book *Quick Ethnography* (2001). The differences correspond to the historical timing of structural change and social transition. In Alaska, increasing interaction between natives and nonnatives coincided with the civil rights movement in the South and provided the impetus for native human and land rights claims through the decade of the 1960s, as well as increasing rates of ethnic violence to children. The subsequent decline of ethnic violence coincides with the establishment of Native Corporations after 1971, which gave natives a position of power in Alaskan society. Collapse of oil prices in the 1980s and other events spurred an increase in ethnic violence to children. Equivalent changes took place in the Russian Far East. The Soviet state maintained firm control over native populations during the height of cold-war tensions in the 1960s and 1970s. Although the incidence of ethnic violence to children remained above 30%, during this period of tight control over native populations it fell from a peak exceeding 50%. In the late 1970s, natives in Kamchatka and Chukotka became increasingly known for their drunkenness. If anything, nonnative views of natives became more negative. During the initial stages of the move toward Glasnost, which raised the possibility of native-nonnative conflicts over resources, the rate of ethnic violence to native children rose once again.

For the Russian Far East we compared these variations in violence inflicted by nonnative authorities on native children with official data on deaths attributable to one or another form of violence (suicides were not counted separately in the Russian data). In Figure 6.3, note the time delay and the close correspondence (90%) of these time series, which were created completely independently, one collected by government and one collected by our research team.

During the decade following the establishment of Native Corporations, nonnative suicide rates rose dramatically, until they began to show evidence of another plateau in the mid-1980s. Suicide rates for native men rose rapidly to exceed by more than two orders of magnitude nonnative Alaskan rates and the aggregate rate for the United States. Among young native men, suicide mortality exceeded the aggregate rate for the U.S. by four to five orders of magnitude.

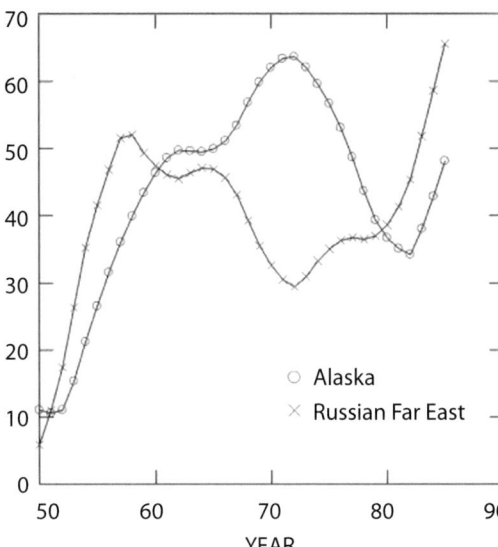

Figure 6.2 Historical variation in emotional violence experienced by native children in Alaska and the Russian Far East (median age = 10 years)

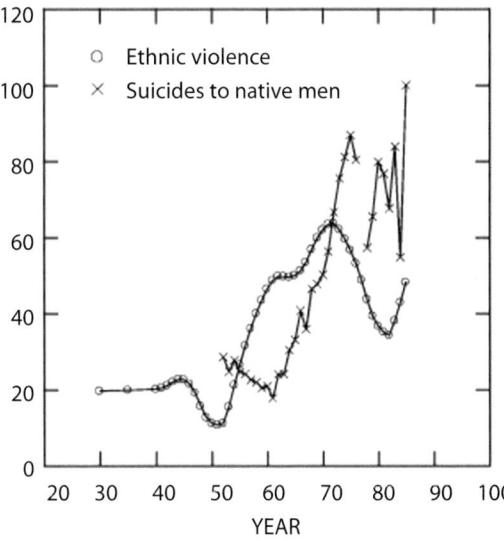

Figure 6.3 Historical variation in emotional violence experienced by native children in Alaska and native suicide rates 9 years later (Pearson's $r = .890$, $p < .000$)

For Alaska we compared these variations in violence inflicted by nonnative authorities on native children with official data on deaths attributable specifically to suicide. Once we close the time delay, note the close correspondence (90%) of these time series (Figure 6.4) created completely independently, one collected by government and one collected by our research team.

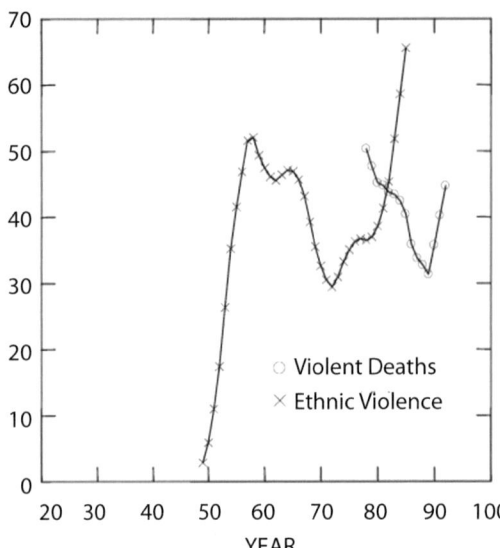

Figure 6.4 Historical variation in emotional violence experienced by native children in the Russian Far East and native suicide rates 13 years later (Pearson's $r = .893$, $p < .000$)

In short, traumatic stress in the form of hurtful words hurled at native children by nonnatives—to whom the prevailing culture assigned the status of authority—led to the "impotent rage" described earlier and to suicide in the face of impossible odds. As nice a description of learned helplessness as I've found.

The same people who make up our cultural communities count simultaneously as our most dangerous threat.

Chapter 7

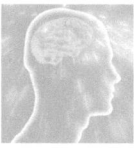

Intelligence Makes for Disturbing Irony

*Insisting on "Fairness" Prods Us to Kill—
Others, Ourselves, or Sometimes Both*

Human evolution produced a culture-creating and culture-dependent creature with a mind that generates a continual flow of innovations and uncertainties, who depends for its well-being on cooperation with other like creatures. Evolved cognitive biases ensure behavioral compliance with the moral vision implicit in a culture's fundamental premises.

The fact remains: the group speculations we call cultural assumptions and the group findings about the moral vision these assumptions yield are as prone to error as the individual minds from which they came. Accepting the power of the cultural consensus will kill you quickly if it takes you in the wrong direction at the wrong time. If you hold to your original assumptions, consistent criticism from cultural authorities will induce in you one or another form of learned helplessness.

Moreover, it takes two to cooperate. Depending on cultures, one of the parties may rule out any options other than control over you or your death, if you cannot otherwise be controlled. Violence, of course, comes in forms that include school-yard bullying and stalking, the battering of women and children, shootings, stabbings, and assaults, and organized warfare and terror attacks. Even for survivors, violence-induced trauma shortens lives and lasts a lifetime. Trauma that induces health problems or critical shifts in behavioral patterns in survivors comes either from dramatic forms of violence (being shot or witnessing someone being killed) or by violence made dramatic because it arrived as a signal from a cultural authority. The latter may include racism, job discrimination, discriminatory school-yard bullying, and community disadvantage.

As discussed in Chapter 5, our propensity to err means that intelligence cannot evolve without a mechanism to differentiate the things of our imagination with empirical content from mistakes, without empirical content—hence, the selective importance of a stress mechanism. By assigning emotional weights to the consequences of behavior for a person's ability to survive and eat well reliably, our brains exert a selective effect by identifying knowledge and reasoning imperfections, which alters the values that apply to a set of choice alternatives. But these emotional weights don't tell us the risks involved in making a specific choice. Intelligence and the cognitive biases discussed in the previous chapter thus required the coevolution of still another property of mind, one that, in the presence of individual survival threats, alters our assessment of the consequences of one choice or another. We're here today, in short, because we evolved a mechanism that differentiates when to go along from when to go it alone. We call this "choice frames."

Let's return to one of the existential questions our ancestors had to answer well consistently—What's best: to share with this person or kill him/her? The answer turns on our ability to negotiate fair treatment in the form of mutual dependencies. We share when we do. And, when and the extent to which we do, cultures act to achieve coherent goals. We resist, sometimes violently, when we can't negotiate those dependencies.

Herein lies the irony. Human minds obsessed with fairness evolved to keep us alive and thriving. Keeping our part of the bargain may require us to kill ourselves. Insisting that others keep their part of the bargain may require us to kill them.

> *Fairness Means "That which is hateful to you, do not do to your fellow . . ."*
> *That is the whole Torah; the rest is the explanation; go and learn. (Hillel the Elder, c. 100 B.C.)*

We come into this world with minds that tell us that we have an inalienable right to fair treatment from our fellow humans.

That claim may provoke furrowed brows and emotional turmoil. After all, how can we know? Don't each of us define "fair" for ourselves? Based on our personal assumptions? Which means, certainly, that there can be no such thing as a universal definition of "fair." And, if so, the claim tells us nothing. Right?

Not quite.

Any review of commentary on "fairness" or "justice" quickly reveals a morass of complexities. Wikipedia's entry on Justice (http://en.wikipedia.org/wiki/Justice) provides a quick glimpse. But such a review also shows that the complexities arise from self-inflicted unasked questions. Like: do we come into the world with an evolved sense of fairness? How is it that so many of us, with no obvious connections, come to agree on what counts as "fair"? How is it that people who we'd think agree with us turn out to radically disagree?

We answered these questions earlier. Morality, our sense of what counts as fair and just, our sense of right and wrong, came into being as an evolutionary by-product of intelligence. Every culture rests on a specific set of speculations. Speculations about the nature of reality imply a specific moral order for each specific behavioral domain. So, what counts as fairness and the application of justice corresponds to the assumptions that ground the culture you apply to a specific behavioral domain.

All of us thus differentiate fair from unfair with two criteria. First, our minds tell us that we, if no one else, come into the world with an unalienable right to life, which only the owning mind may disavow. Second, our minds tell us that behavior should conform to the moral vision that specific postulates imply for a given behavioral realm. Dissonance between the two—moral vision and behavior—alters how we frame choices.

What If You Don't Buy Into a Given Culture?

> *We are told from all sides that if one wins a lethal encounter, he will feel dreadful. It is odd that no one seems to have felt dreadful about this until very recently. Throughout recorded history the winning of a fight has generally been considered a subject for congratulation. It is only just now that it has become presumably tainted. . . . a predatory felon who victimizes innocent noncombatants on the streets is a proven goblin, sentenced by his own initiative. Some men may be upset by killing him, but not anyone I have met.*
> *(Col. Jeff Cooper;* To Ride, Shoot Straight, and Speak the Truth, *2005, pp. 24–26)*

Because meaning comes from our starting assumptions, an event that traumatizes one person who interprets experience based on one set of cultural assumptions – will not traumatize another person—who interprets experience based on an alternative set of cultural assumptions. Hurtful words can't affect people who use another culture. If you follow the honor culture of the American South, no threats by your neighbors will make you kill the women, whose safety counts as your most important job. If you follow the honor culture of the Middle East and South Asia, no threats by your neighbors will make you not kill the women who threaten the family, whose safety counts as your most important job.

What counts as fair depends on the cultural assumptions that ground a specific moral vision. Clashes of cultures count as one the more important facts of human life. What makes clashing cultures problematic is our mind's insistence that we deserve fair treatment from other humans even when our cultures differ.

This matches much of real life. We negotiate our way daily through multiple cultural environments, only some of which we count as "ours." Our minds keep us acutely attuned to how others, including people who adhere to other cultures, respond to what we do

Figure 7.1

or do not do. As far as the culture is concerned, the only thing that matters is the extent that you do what the people on a given cultural team expect. Behavioral compliance does not, of course, mean you have to "believe in" the norms. You may, indeed, agree with a given set of cultural facts and norms. The Dallas Cowboys are "America's Team," "Black" Americans are "Democrats" and those who aren't, like (for example) Supreme Court Justice Clarence Thomas, or Frederick Douglass, count as traitors to their race. Well, maybe not all. Some (Robert Griffen, III) just don't count as "real" black men.

But you may not care one way or another. You may, in fact, disagree sharply. To you, football may count merely as a game for boys who failed to grow up. Although, for some of you, "gun control" means controlling the movement of guns between people, for others it means controlling the movement of a gun while you shoot it.

Because we experience—at least indirectly—sanctions for violations of norms in cultures other than our own, we may obsess over how others may see and respond to what we do. Should (for example) a newspaper post the photo of Winston Churchill as is, with the cigar, or should it avoid controversy by photoshopping the cigar away? Maybe you should keep to yourself the thought that it makes no sense to you that men who have sex when drunk are exploiters and women who have sex when drunk are victims. What words or actions should *you* avoid? And why? Indeed, without clarity about the assumptions that produce your norms, you will feel pulled in multiple directions. (Some people obsess over these conflicts more than others do, of course. There's now a web page to help those of you who seriously obsess over not agreeing with or not doing what others think you should agree with or do: http://www.wikihow.com/Not-Care-What-People-Think.)

We all know about and participate, at least on the periphery and by implication, in many, many cultures not "our own." So long as we feel treated reasonably fairly, as Timur Kuran observed in his 1995 book *Private Truths, Public Lies*, we uphold our end of the fairness bargain and go along with whatever cultural consensus we face.

Unfair treatment creates dissonance, and a dilemma. If we acknowledge and thereby validate the cultural authority, we acknowledge to ourselves that we confused fair-but-bad treatment with unfair treatment. Bad treatment that's fair means we screwed up. Enough "fair-but-bad" treatment leads us to question our right to life, and we "learn helplessness." As we saw in Chapter 6, learned helplessness elicits suicide, by one means or another.

Because cultural authorities count as legitimate only by reference to a specific set of cultural assumptions, legitimacy shifts elsewhere when you change assumptions. Illegitimacy eliminates the power of a culture to hurt you with words, although the culture still may possess means to physically threaten you. Consequently, under some circumstances, it's prudent to "keep your head down."

Resistance of whatever kind, however, requires you to act on the norms of another culture. Action makes clashing cultural assumptions explicit. Once you insist that other people with clashing cultures keep their part of the fairness bargain that binds us together as human beings, you face simple choices. Negotiate good behavior or enforce it. To treat your cultural team members fairly, enforcement may require you to kill yourself (Masada, Saipan, Jonestown), to offer your life for your team members (Ayat al-Akhras, who blew herself up in an Israeli supermarket in 2002; or the Marine Cpl. Kyle Carpenter, who threw himself on a grenade to save his friend while on combat duty in Afghanistan in 2010), which may occur while you seek to kill those who, by not fulfilling the human fairness bargain, show themselves as not human (the young Oklahoma mother who shot and killed an intruder on New Year's Eve to protect her 3-month old baby). Fighting back, defending yourself, empowerment, or whatever term you prefer, consists of a series of discrete choices. We may frame a choice by focusing on what we might lose or by what we might gain. Our minds inflate the risk involved in making a choice if we focus on potential gains. Our minds deflate the risk involved in making a choice if we focus on potential losses. The outcome is a cognitive bias that makes us hate losses more than we love gains. Evolutionarily significant threats—to our life, to our reproductive capacity, for example—elicit choice frames that focus on losses.

The Evolution of Choice Frames

Given an intelligent form of life, selection had to favor the evolution of a mechanism that weights choice consequences (*ES*) by the change they produce, in the likelihood that an organism will avoid death, eat well reliably, and thus optimize its reproductive success. Selection necessarily gives priority to short-run success and thus must also favor a mechanism that weights the severity (*S*) of a consequence by its immediacy

(*I*) and certainty (*C*). Consequences that do not occur immediately introduce uncertainty, measured as certainty weighted by immediacy. The evolutionary significance (*ES*) of a consequence thus consists of a severity metric weighted by the immediacy and uncertainty of *S*: $ES = S*I*(I*C)$. In short, the evolutionary significance of a choice consequence changes with increases in the inherent threat of a consequence given (a) increases in both the immediacy and certainty of the consequence, (b) increases in the immediacy but decreases in the certainty of the consequence, and (c) decreases in the immediacy but increases in the certainty of the consequence. Imagine that each variable exhibits values between 0 and 1. *ES* metrics over 0.5 must reflect consequence severity of at least 0.6 and very high levels of immediacy and certainty. *ES* metrics over 0.5 thus identify consequences that may significantly decrease the likelihood that an organism will survive well if at all. Ambiguity in the immediacy or certainty of the consequence thus sends no error signal.

Human relationships exhibit dynamics that vary with the relative power of the actors. *Power* (following Max Weber) is the ability to influence or control the behavior and beliefs of others even without their consent. Power comes from the capacity of one person to inflict evolutionarily significant consequences on another. The capacity to inflict these consequences accrues to any individual or organization to the extent to which it serves as gatekeeper for access to means of survival and resource access for clients. Power grows with the importance of the resources involved and the number of clients.

Equality characterizes a relationship when neither social actor depends on the other for survival and resource access, or when both depend on the other equally. Mutual dependence equality is characterized by equal capacities to inflict evolutionarily significant consequences on the other. Sanctions in the form of costly punishments may have coevolved with the propensity to cooperate. Thus the common assumption that weakness elicits violence and strength deters it may come from a mind evolved to respond sensitively to variations in the immediacy and certainty with which a consequence bears on life, reliable access to food, and reproductive success. When social actors can respond (tit-for-tat) with equivalent consequences, maximum survivability comes from keeping *ES* below 0.5. Selection thus favors the evolution of a mechanism that frames behavioral choices as gains and links this choice frame with an exaggerated sense of risks. Behavioral choices that focus on gains thus avoid interactions in which *ES* > 0.5, because choice makers fear losing something they worked hard to acquire. Equals consequently engage in risk aversion strategies and, in general and on balance, treat each other well. Because equals rarely violate behavior norms in significant ways, equalities produce stability in social relations. Among equals, consequently, selection operates only weakly on moral clarity regarding the parameters of acceptable and unacceptable behavior and, thus, the ability to identify and (attempt to) maintain behavioral boundaries. The individuals most likely to surprise you with offensive and threatening behavior are those you think of as friends.

We thus share when we have reason to think we will receive fair treatment. Fair treatment comes when individuals are careful, to borrow a phrase from Hillel the Elder, to not do to their fellow that which is hateful to them. Unfair treatment comes from individuals who treat you in ways that you find hateful.

Others will treat you in ways you find hateful if and when their acts elicit no signal of error.

Exploitation Calls for Resistance

Equality shifts to inequality as the capacity to inflict evolutionarily significant consequences on other people emerges and grows. Powerful people maximize their survivability by maintaining or increasing their capacity to inflict evolutionarily significant consequences on others. As ES_{max} falls for one social actor, however, selection favors the evolution of a mechanism that shifts choices framed (cautiously) as gains to choices framed as losses and links these losses to a mechanism that decreases the weight of perceived negative outcomes in direct proportion to the evolutionary significance of the choice. Therefore, as ES_{max} differences grow, behavioral choices consequences become increasingly irrelevant to powerful people who develop a growing sense of entitlement. As power differences grow larger, the fair behavior that characterizes interaction between equals shifts increasingly rapidly to increasingly exploitative and eventually violent behavior. Unlimited agency creates killers.

For observers or clients of authorities, the *halo effect* mentioned in Chapter 5 widens the realm of action over which a person or things with authority exercises authority, in the sense that he/she/it influences what you do even without your consent. For people who count as authorities in a specific culture, the halo effect transforms the praise, admiration, and deference we receive from others into an essential component of our sense of self as a superior being. Authorities find themselves doing more and more things without any sense of consequences. Power corrupts and absolute power corrupts absolutely, because our minds transform the absence of consequences into the postulate that we enjoy, even if no one else does—an unalienable right to do anything we might enjoy. Deference becomes the expected due of the powerful, and the absence of deference counts as a threat—which elicits defensive action that, from the point of view of the nondeferent, counts as corruption and violence.

As the *ES* metrics that powerless people experience grow larger than 0.5, clients search increasingly intensively for alternative resource access channels to counter the power of gatekeepers. Inequalities thus generate instability. So long as people frame their behavioral choices as involving gains and *ES* remains < 0.5, tit-for-tat behavioral responses keep exploitative behavior within bounds. However, once *ES* grows beyond 0.5, people fear the loss of something that constitutes their (human) right and experience anger, if not outrage, if their entitlements are not met. As *ES* grows, both powerful and powerless people discount at increasing rates the risks they undertake to defend themselves. Because a shopkeeper confronted by an armed robber risks death whether or not he or she grabs

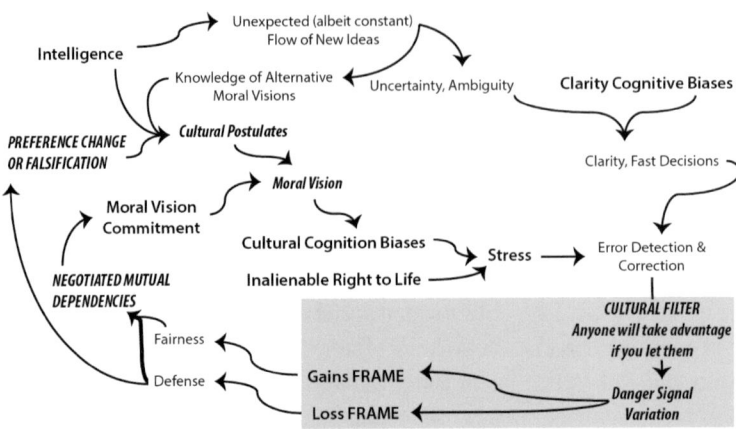

Figure 7.2

a gun to stop the assailant, for example, grabbing the gun adds so little to the immediate threat that it doesn't count. Power inequalities fall as the number or importance of alternative resource access channels grows. Growth in the ES_{max} of relatively powerless people elicits nonlinear growth in powerful people's exploitative and violent behavior, which declines once the ES_{max} of formerly powerless people exceeds .5. Theoretically as well as empirically, and for both state and individual actors, weakness thus elicits predation and strength deters it. As inequalities grow, the increase in violence exposure induces selection for moral clarity about behavioral boundaries and dehumanization of the "other." People count as fellow humans to the extent to which they treat each other fairly. Our minds transition out of the category of "fellow human" anyone who fails this test; the distance between fellow human and enemy grows with the predation threat. Both /Twi and Padlu (Chapter 4), for example, acted to defend their existing prerogatives. To others, their prerogatives counted as exploitative behavior—behavior judged unfair by virtue of cultural norms. Negotiated mutual dependencies must include limits on one's agency. Violations of cultural norms not signaled clearly produce only more egregious violations. Quick, certain, and deadly serious sanctions send clear signals—which explains why their respective communities in the Kalahari and the Arctic heartedly approved when ≠Gau killed /Twi and Qijuk killed Padlu. Moreover, people who grow up in traumatic/violent (exploitative) cultural environments should learn to be highly sensitive to power relations, to respond quickly and strongly when others attempt to take advantage of them, and, in order to minimize the chance of further exploitation, to search harder than others for ways to avoid dependency.

Yes. Lord Acton (and Whoever First Observed That "a Fish Rots from the Head") Was Right All Along

Our mind's propensity to shift choice frames from gains to losses in the presence of unfair treatment explains why the premise that strength deters violence and weakness elicits it lies at the heart of Sun Tzu's 2,500-year-old *The Art of War*, Machiavelli's *The Prince*, Beccaria's *On Crimes and Punishments* and rationalizes nearly all international, domestic, and personal violence prevention policies. A widely shared personal policy in American culture, for example, holds that individuals should avoid 'dangerous situations,' meaning situations in which one makes oneself 'vulnerable,' because they send a signal of weakness to potential predators. It follows, and we tell children, to stay away from strangers and not to talk with them or get in their car. We tell women not to go out alone; while they're out we urge them to avoid distractions (cell phones, searching purse), to walk with authority and purpose (don't look scared); that, if approached, to look the person in the eyes (to signal alertness), talk with the person (to signal that you can identify them); and, if attacked, to yell, (threaten to) fight back, and carry something with which to fight back effectively. Consistently, people frame a choice to defend, even if only in a trivial way, as a loss. Listen to people talk about situations in which they acted to "defend" themselves:

> Remark at dinner, wife to husband: "If you take my bread, I'll hurt you." (pers. comm.)

> A 26-year-old man recalls: "I was 10 years old, and the neighboring Tajik kid living across the street from me was 8 years old. We often played together, and I used to pick on him and bully him around a lot, just for the fun of it. It was a boy thing. . . . I liked being the older, bigger one and the leader, so when we played games, I set the rules and he had to oblige. I guess the kid got tired of my bossing him around, and when he turned 9 years old, he thought he could confront me. He got a little bit bigger at 9, and cockier. He confronted me one day. We started arguing about something silly, when he got into my face saying, 'Wanna fight? Wanna fight?' I told him, 'Let's fight later. Meet me here at the same spot later, and we will fight, if that's what you want.' I went home and told my older brothers what happened. I was apprehensive, and I didn't want to fight, but my brothers got me pumped to fight the kid. Also, I was thinking, 'If I choose not to fight, then it's the same as having this kid automatically win.' If I didn't fight, I knew he would then be the bully of me." (pers. comm.)

> A woman in her mid-30s explains, "With an intruder in your home at a time when they know you are there, you can assume they don't just want your stuff. I would assume the worst and take action to prevent death." (pers. comm.)

According to a 38-year-old man, "I hit [women] when I can't get through to them [communicate my point of view] no other way. I would beat women not because I am a man and they are a woman, but because it irritates me to the fullest when I can't get through verbally." (pers. comm.)

Figure 7.3 shows what we might expect from an empirical study. As the evolutionary significance of consequences grows, violence rates should fall at rates that vary with the likelihood that people frame choices as losses. As the *ES* metric rises, populations characterized by minimal inequalities (and a very low likelihood that people frame choices as losses) should exhibit an increasing rate of decline in violence, whereas populations characterized by severe inequalities (and a very high likelihood that people frame choices as losses) should exhibit a decreasing rate of decline in violence. Figure 7.3 exhibits projections consistent with a series of studies in Barbados and Antigua in the late 20th century. Weakness elicited violence, and people subject to childhood violence evolved behavioral mechanisms that reduced the likelihood of finding themselves subject to violence as adults.

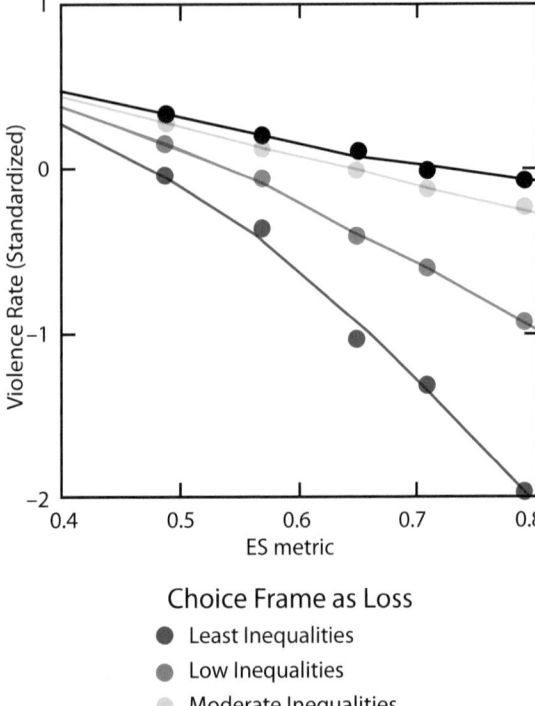

Figure 7.3 Simulated rates of violence by the evolutionary significance of consequences, the credibility of which varies with prevalent inequalities and the likelihood that people frame choices as losses

First, West Indian data consistently show that power inequalities between domestic partners (for example, where women have little income, no significant income-generating skills, and few or no relatives or friends to help them) elicit violence toward women and their children; conversely, power equalities between partners elicit affectionate and supportive behavior for women and their children, irrespective of class, education, or the presence of stepfathers in the home. A 1998 study of the combined Barbadian and Antiguan data (Why Violence?, published in the journal of the Society for Applied Anthropology, *Human Organization*) pointed out further that as gender power inequalities decrease, the chances that even rotten men act affectionately grows by a factor of 9 (from .057 to .512), and the chances that they act violently falls by more than 50% (from .889 to .412). Moreover, power corrupts even good men. As gender power inequalities grow, the chances that even good men act affectionately falls 75% (from .813 to .200), and the chances that they act violently grows by a factor of 4.6 (from .145 to .660). Similarly, people subject to violence, particularly during childhood, evolve behavioral patterns that reduce their chances of becoming subject to violence as adults.

Both Barbados and Antigua exhibited what we can fairly characterize as a culture of violence prior to major structural change in the regional economies. As elsewhere in the West Indies, not only was battering a culturally acceptable practice, men occasionally asserted *droit de seigneur* rights to daughters. More than half the people interviewed reported that his or her mother experienced significant levels of emotional and physical violence. Approximately 1 in 4 experienced childhood emotional and physical violence. On Barbados, nearly 1 in 3 women experienced childhood sexual violence. Opportunities for West Indian women to escape dependence on men and on childbearing increased dramatically after the mid-1960s, as the economy shifted from an emphasis on agriculture to an emphasis on tourism. Most new job opportunities required high levels of educational and technical skills. The expansion of employment opportunities drew women into school and pushed them farther than they would have gone otherwise. Women used their education to take advantage of the new employment opportunities in increasing numbers. Women who empowered themselves in this way experienced from their partners far more domestic help, emotional support, and affectionate behavior than women who did not—and little or no family violence. Women freed from dependency on childbearing had fewer children. Women simultaneously freed from dependency on men enjoyed markedly better relationships with their partners. The incidence of family violence fell dramatically in just one generation. Most important (see details in this chapter's Appendix Table 1—*we find no cycle of violence effects among men married to powerful women.*

Second, variation in sexual cultures corresponds with variation in a woman's experience with traumatic/violent and supportive/affectionate cultural environments. Women in Barbados who grew up in households marked by affection and support began sexual activity relatively late, had relatively few partners and few or no sexually transmitted diseases (STDs), experienced good relationships with their current partner, and were subject to little sexual or gender-based harassment later in life. By contrast, Barbadian women who grew up in households marked by gender inequalities experienced sexual, physical, and emotional violence toward women and children. This exploitative childhood environment corresponded with an early start to sexual activity with much older first partners and, in adolescence, high levels of childbearing as well as a pattern of high sexual mobility that continued through their early 30s. Catherine Fuentes reported similar patterns among American women in her 2008 "Pathways" article in the *Journal of Women's Health.*

Data from Antigua, moreover, allowed us to express concretely the contrasting effects of exploitative or nonexploitative childhood environments for two hypothetical sets of girls. Both sets initiated sexual activity at age 12, and both engaged only in visiting relationships with men through age 20. The model predictions reveal that exploited Antiguan women invested in childbearing both more and less than women who grew up in exploitation-free homes, depending on ecological contingencies. Girls who grew up in exploitation-free homes acquired four different sexual partners, achieved O-level passes (or close to it), and averaged about one child by age 20 when job opportunities were low, and O-level or A-level passes, and about one child, once job opportunities rose. Girls who experienced intense exploitation (including nonincestuous sexual predation at age 12), by contrast, acquired seven different partners by age 20 and averaged six to ten years of schooling and two children by age 20 when job opportunities were low. Girls with the same experiences achieved A-level passes and a year or two of college (15 years of schooling) and no children, once job opportunities rose. Antiguan women who experienced sexual predation thus used a pattern of sexual mobility not only to reduce their dependence on any one partner but also as a means to supersede the limitations on their educational achievements imposed by their history of exploitation. The finding that the number of sexual partners neither increases nor decreases the educational achievements of unmolested women confirms that a history of exploitation alters gender relationships in fundamental ways. High sexual mobility counts as one means that exploited women use to empower themselves.

"An Armed Society Is a Polite Society" (Robert Heinlein)

In short, yes, deterrents consist of an ability to inflict evolutionarily significant consequences on anyone who fails to hold up his or her end of the human bargain to treat others fairly.

But.

Deterrent credibility (and effects) varies with whether people frame choices as gains or losses.

Figure 7.4 shows violent crime rates for the United States between 2001 and 2004, given specific values for variables that bear on the evolutionary significance of a consequence and its credibility. If evolved properties of mind provide the means by which we respond to the world of experience, the immediacy with which a consequence bears on survival, eating well reliably, and reproductive success should determine the design of choice alternatives and the costs of their consequences, which we ordinarily call the *balance of power* in a relationship. Significant and quick consequences should deter violence. A low risk of significant and quick consequences should increase violence. Relatively insignificant and slow consequences should also increase violence. These behavioral trends should reflect the degree to which population frame their choices as losses. (The Appendix at the end of this chapter provides details of the variables and the modes of analysis.)

Here's the short story. We measured Choices Framed as Losses with information on the size of populations plausibly subject to exploitative dependencies. We measured the likelihood of consequences with information on small-world properties of specific populations (h/t Russ Bernard) and the cost of consequences with information on the availability of means of defense useful even for small, physically weak, elderly, or disabled people. We checked these results with information on things like household income, Gini coefficients, and the size of the local prison population.

The finding? Violent crimes go up when the likelihood and cost of consequences—as measured by small-world properties and the availability of guns—goes down. Study the effect of the

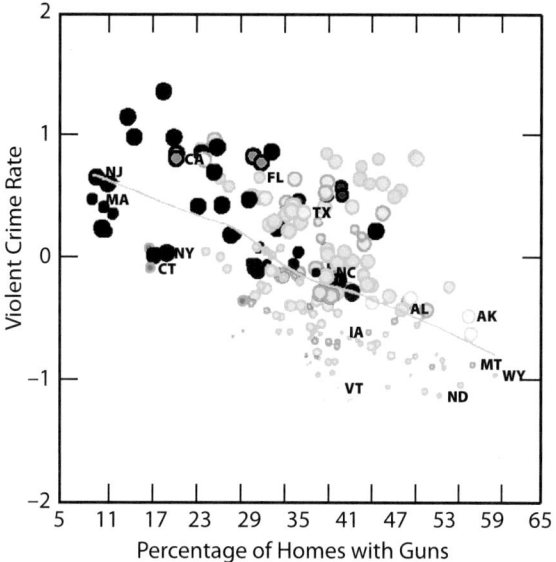

Figure 7.4 LOWESS smoothed relationship (2001–2004) between violent crime rates in the United States (factor scores) and the percentage of homes with guns and CCW access (standardized). Symbol size is proportional to the size of sanction devaluation populations. Selected states appear as abbreviations (AL, AK, CT, FL, IA, MA, MT, NC, ND, NJ, NY, TX, VT, and WY). Black symbols identify states that issue gun permits rarely and highly selectively; gray symbols identify states that issue gun permits upon request (AK and VT do not require permits).

prevalence of loss choice frames, shown as high by large symbols and low by small symbols. Note that a high prevalence of loss choice frames corresponds with levels of violent crime higher than warranted solely by the prevalence of small world properties and effective means of defense.

The Bottom Line?

Inequality is the Root of Social Evil. (Pope Francis, 4:28 a.m., 28 April 2014)

Human evolution produced a culture-creating and culture-dependent creature with a mind that generates a continual flow of innovations and uncertainties, who depends for its well-being on cooperation with other like creatures. Evolved cognitive biases ensure behavioral compliance with the moral vision implicit in a culture's fundamental premises—assuming that people treat each other fairly. If they don't, our choice frames bias shifts from a focus on gains to a focus on losses. This choice frame shift makes explicit cultural conflicts and, with or without violence, produces cultural changes.

Why? Because, just like climate change, which produced agriculture and both created and brought down civilizations, and like changes in the size, composition, location of populations, which produced equivalent changes, explicit cultural conflicts change the consequences of choices. Cultures don't change otherwise.

Want to reduce violent crime? Make it possible for individuals to negotiate fair behavior from others—increase small-world properties, effective means of self-defense, and opportunities to escape exploitation.

Appendix to Chapter 7

Part 1

Table 7.1 reports as yet unpublished findings of a multiple logistic regression test for social learning "cycle of violence" effects among 344 of these posttransition men and women in Barbados. The binary dependent variable integrates emotional and physical violence because both consistently appeared together. Post hoc tests for the effects of potential confounders—whether main effects, poverty and social status, SES-based strains between partners, social learning, or family and personal histories— show effects best explained by chance.

Some findings appear unsurprising as well as theoretically uninteresting. Men who reported emotional abuse from their partner, for example, reported the odds of treating their partner violently nearly 24 times more often than the odds of violence by men who reported no such emotional abuse. Women who traded sex for drugs reported elevated rates of violence, as did women in long-duration unions. The latter reflected a tendency among the oldest women in the Barbadian sample to have been subject to violence earlier in life.

Some findings appear theoretically interesting but unsurprising considering earlier studies. Women who could not count on interventions from their sons or brother or father reported the odds of violence 10 times higher than the odds reported by women who could count on those interventions, for example. Similarly, women without the personal power that comes from well-paying employment based on high educational achievement reported odds of violence about 3.6 times higher than the odds for women with such power. The finding that the likelihood of violence falls with the degree of affection a woman receives from her partner provides further support for the "rotten man" hypothesis. The finding that sexual mobility reduces a woman's exposure to violence from her partner provides further support for the empowering effects of sexual behavior.

Some findings appear both surprising and theoretically interesting. We see one widely reported social learning effect—for example, that women who were abused by their mothers reported higher levels of abuse than women who grew up in a supportive

Table 1. Determinants of Violence Toward Women Among Post-Transition Men & Women, Barbados

DEPENDENT VAR: **Abused**			95.0% BOUNDS			
PARAMETER	ODDS	RATIO	UPPER	LOWER	T	P
Woman a Man Reports as Emotionally Abusive	I	23.747	339.152	1.663	2.335	0.020
No Intervention Assistance for Dependent Woman	I	10.118	23.878	4.287	5.283	0.000
Woman Without Personal Power from Educational Achievements and Employment Success	I	3.565	6.957	1.827	3.727	0.000
Women Who Were Abused by their Mothers	I	2.842	6.591	1.226	2.435	0.015
Sexual Partners for Women Involved with Drugs	I	1.249	1.426	1.094	3.293	0.001
Powerless Women in Relationships with Men Abused by Abused Mothers	I	1.145	1.290	1.016	2.217	0.027
Woman in Union of Long Duration	I	1.085	1.132	1.040	3.758	0.000
Woman Given Affection by her Partner	I	0.890	0.932	0.849	−4.882	0.000
Woman with Many Sexual Partners	I	0.860	0.958	0.771	−2.734	0.006

$2*[LL(N)-LL(0)] = 142.426$ WITH 9 DOF, CHI-SQ P-VALUE = 0.000

Log-Likelihood Tests Of the H0:βk=0.00 for all Control Variables				
	Unrestricted			
Main Effects	LL	DF	Chi-sq	P
	146.881	15	4.455	.814
	Unrestricted			
Poverty and Social Status	LL	DF	Chi-sq	P
	144.844	14	2.418	.789
Lower class home, Woman's job status, Partner's job status, Woman's educational level, Partner's educational level				
	Unrestricted			
Socioeconomic Strains	LL	DF	Chi-sq	P
	142.457	13	0.031	.999
Difference in job status, Difference in educational level, Difference in job status for People in the lower class, Difference in educational level for people in the lower class				
	Unrestricted			
Social Learning	LL	DF	Chi-sq	P
	148.115	20	5.689	.893
MEN AND WOMEN: Childhood abuse by mother's partner, MEN ONLY: Childhood abuse by mother MEN AND WOMEN: Abuse to mother by mother's partner, MEN AND WOMEN: Affection toward mother MEN AND WOMEN: Affection from mother's partner, MEN AND WOMEN: Affection from mother				
	Unrestricted			
Family & Personal History	LL	DF	Chi-sq	P
	147.755	23	4.101	.995
Age, Raised in a stable nuclear family household, Raised in a home with a stepfather Raised by foster parents, Raised by a mother with no (regular) partner, Raised in a lower class home Frequency of illicit drug use, Number of different sexual partners				

childhood environment. We do not, however, see an unconditional cycle-of-violence effect among abused men. Men abused by their father did not by virtue of that experience inflict violence on their partner. Men whose father abused their mother likewise did not by virtue of that experience inflict violence on their partner. Men whose father abused their mother who subjected their sons to violence abused their partners—but *only when the partner relationship exhibited significant inequalities.*

Part 2

If evolved properties of mind provide the means by which we respond to the world of experience, the immediacy with which a consequence bears on survival, eating well reliably, and reproductive success should determine the design of choice alternatives and the costs of their consequences, which we ordinarily call the *balance of power* in a relationship. Significant and quick consequences should deter violence. A low risk of significant and quick consequences should increase violence. Relatively insignificant and slow consequences should also increase violence.

The following test of these hypotheses uses a pooled state-level cross-sectional (50 states), four-year time series for the years 2001–2004 concerning the incidence of three kinds of violence in the United States: murder and nonnegligent homicide, robbery, and aggravated assaults. The dependent variable comes from FBI Uniform Crime Reports. I imputed the occasional missing datum by assigning the average for all states with no missing values. State and year specific crime rates measure incident reports relative to CDC population estimates. All forms of violent crime (murder, robbery, aggravated assault, with or without firearms) fluctuate together over space and time and constitute a unitary cultural phenomenon. A principal components analysis of the various violent crime rates revealed a single factor (factor 1 explained 81.64% of the matrix variance and its eigenvalue was 8.4 times larger than the eigenvalue for factor 2). Using only one of the variables that constitute a multidimensional phenomenon such as violent crime introduces measurement error or, perhaps, measurement bias. The dependent variable for this study thus consists of the factor scores derived from this analysis ($\sigma = .768$).

The following analysis looks at the effects on violent crime rates of three classes of variables: those that (1) measure the properties of social networks that reduce or increase the likelihood of detection and punishment, (2) measure cultural variation in the assessment of punishment severity, and (3) measure cultural variation in the speed of detection and punishment severity. These variables constitute "superorganic" properties of human populations in the sense meant by Alfred Kroeber: they constitute properties of the environments in which people live, that affect our lives however much we might want to wish them away.

Small world environmental properties, like neighbors or authorities who intensively monitor behavior (for instance, the former Soviet Union, contemporary Japan), increase the immediacy and certainty of sanctions of a given severity. Short-term

TABLE 2. Hierarchical Linear Mixed Model Analysis (random intercept and slopes): Violent Crime in the United States, 2001–2004 (AIC: 106.591)

	Effect Coefficient	95% CL	
		Lower	Upper
Intercept	0.000		
Proportion of Population in Urban Areas	0.879	0.727	1.131
Ln (Small World Properties*CCW Access)	–0.044	–0.079	–0.009
Percentage of Homes with Guns	–0.011	–0.014	–0.008
Young (18–29) Minority Men (standardized)*Guns	0.013	0.010	0.016
Poor, Unemployed, Uneducated Men (factor scores)* CCW	0.059	0.046	0.073

Test for Main Effects, YMM: t=0.033, p=.973; PUU: t=0.000, p=1.000; CCW: t=-0.012, p=.990; SW: t= -0.021, p=.983. For Included main effects, AIC = 114.598. Substitution of main effects for the interaction terms increases the AIC score nearly 16 points to 122.546. AIC equals 122.432 if we eliminate the large-world variable, 283.001 if we eliminate the credibility/choice frame variables, and 149.391 if we eliminate the ES variables.

Test for Controls (entered one at a time): Supply of Perpetrators (Male Prison Population as a Proportion of Total): t=-1.102, p=.272; Poverty (Median Income): t=0.033, p=.974; Social and Economic Inequities (Proportion of Population Black/African American: t=.0.565, p=.573; GINI coefficients: t=-0.009, t= .995; Difference between White and Minority Per Capita Income: t=-.016, p=.987).

memory limitations imply that the maximum size of face-to-face networks approximates 140 people (Bernard and Killworth 1973). Nonetheless, huge numbers of people organized in many localized clusters over great distances may be connected by a small number of ties to create small worlds in which members experience great connectedness. High levels of connectedness and the sense of belonging that it elicits mean a higher likelihood that breaches of behavioral norms will be identified and sanctioned. Low levels of connectedness and the sense of anonymity that it elicits mean a lower likelihood that breaches of behavioral norms will be identified and sanctioned. Population compression creates new network ties that may produce only small changes in the degree of clustering but dramatic declines in the average distance between network members (Watts and Strogatz 1998). Population density relative to population size thus measures small-world properties that should increase the certainty of immediate sanctions and predict decreases in violent crime rates.

Environmental properties that increase the likelihood of evolutionarily significant sanctions ($ES > .5$) may consist of friends and family who deter battering by threatening physical intervention (for example, Koss 2000), a practice of swift, consistent incarceration for violation of a restraining order (for instance, 4th District Court, Knox County, TN), or a population of armed citizens (such as Switzerland, Israel). Within the contemporary United States, FBI data for the years 2001–2004 indicate that 60% of murders and nonnegligent homicides, nearly 40% of robberies, and 17% of aggravated assaults involve the use of guns; thus the prevalence of firearms and the ease with which a citizen may acquire them (for example, in the form of licenses for the concealed carry of weapons) may provide an effective way to enforce breaches of behavioral norms quickly.

Death or serious injury constitutes an excessively costly consequence. Even small and physically weak people can and do use a gun to kill or seriously injure predatory attackers. In the United States, people use guns daily to protect themselves effectively (Hahn et al. 2003, Kleck and Gertz 1995, Tark and Kleck 2004).

Data on the proportion of population in urban areas come from the U.S. Census in 2000. The small world (population compression) variable consists of population density relative to population. The armed citizenry variables were formed with data from the CDC and information on the laws and practices pertaining to the issue of licenses for the carry of a concealed weapon (CCW). The CDC's Behavioral Risk Factor Surveillance System provided estimates of the proportion of households with guns. I imputed these missing data with SYSTAT's EM maximum likelihood estimation procedure, once it was determined that missing values in the gun prevalence data were missing completely at random relative to the violent crime variables (Little's MCAR statistic = 2.902, $df = 6, p = .821$). I measured CCW access as 1 for states that "may issue" CCW permits but that do so rarely (such as Massachusetts, New York, New Jersey), 5 for states that "may issue" CCW permits and do so regularly (for instance, Connecticut), 6 for states that "shall issue" CCW permits for any qualified individual who requests one (for example, Florida, Texas), and 10 for Vermont and Alaska, which do not require permits for CCW.

Lessons Learned

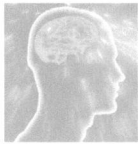

Cultures Aren't Merely Curiosities, and How "Others" Think and Act

How other people think and act may elicit fascination, or other interesting emotions.

- A woman/ghost/village can marry a woman and father her children? You're kidding!!!??? Cool!
- Ouch. Those penis sheaths worn in New Guinea look *very* uncomfortable.
- Love those belly dances!
- They cut off *what* part of a female's genitalia??? Barbaric!!!
- What do you mean, I can't go out in public uncovered and without a male escort?
- When I saw the blood [during the Nuer initiation ceremony in which boys receive marks of Gar] I almost puked. Don't think I could hold it if we saw a film on rites of passage that involved circumcision.

And that predominately remains how we—social scientists included—treat and think about cultural differences. One can use them to illustrate how we're all alike, just different or to illustrate the disastrous effects of globalization or the current favorite "ism," or the dangers of climate change, or the heritage you should (take pride in/be ashamed of), or you name it. But they remain curiosities, and, as (for example) American Indian wannabes who wander onto reservations find out, curiosities aren't real.

Clifford Geertz argued more than 50 years ago in his *Impact of the Concept of Culture on the Concept of Man* that the realities of our individual lives come into being only as cultures construct and run them. This book explains why and how. We evolved and survive, indeed thrive, only because we do not and cannot exist independently of cultures. Individuals can't do anything independently of cultures, and their success or lack of success will reflect the cultures in which they participate.

Any theory that assigns responsibility for events to individuals thus fundamentally misconstrues how the world works. And therein lies the importance of cultural anthropology, as Alfred Kroeber, Leslie White, and others suggested early in the 20th century. As we more precisely work out the implications of this finding, we shall come to understand the properties of cultures that produce (as one example) achievements like The-Man-Who-Saved-a-Billion-Lives) Norman Borlaug's Green Revolution—he showed the way but accomplished the revolution only as leader in a distinctive culture supported by a huge community of peers. We shall thus improve our chances of equivalent future achievements, like those identified by the U.S. National Academy of Engineering or the Grand Challenges in Global Health program.

Meanwhile, consider how a few simpler implications bear on issues like poverty, American rape culture, gun control, conflict analysis and resolution, and racism. Our starting point? Cultures consist of teams of people who, because they ground their understanding of the world on a common postulate about its nature, share a specific moral vision for a behavioral domain. The difference between postulates and the rules/norms/expectations we live by? A postulate makes a claim about the nature of a behavioral domain. Rules/norms/expectations tell you which choice to make.

Distorted Narratives

Things possess no inherent meaning. Meaning comes from the assumptions used to make sense of the thing; anthropological Truism makes nonsense of *all* narratives that assume a thing comes with an inherent meaning. Among the most common and egregious examples? Narratives on poverty, social justice, bullying, and rape.

Immediately before I wrote this sentence I googled the phrase "growing up in poverty" and received 81,000,000 hits. The narratives simplify to: poverty is horrible, with stresses and material limitations that damage the life chances of children and damage adult ability to make good choices. Where to start? Maybe Frederick Douglass, born into slavery sometime around 1818, who freed himself and by 1845 emerged as a nationally celebrated orator, writer, and statesman. Or Thomas Sowell, born in 1930 North Carolina to a widowed mother, moved to Harlem at age 9, forced by finances and family troubles to drop out of school by age 17, worked at a series of entry-level jobs until he was drafted in 1951 but graduated from Harvard *magna cum laude* in 1958, received his Ph.D. in economics from the University of Chicago in 1968, and authored (among many publications) nearly 40 books between 1972 and 2013. Or Clarence Thomas, born in 1948 Georgia to a farm worker father and domestic worker mother whose first language was Gullah, who didn't enjoy regular meals or indoor plumbing until his family moved into the Savannah home of his maternal grandfather, when Thomas was 7, who made himself an honor student as the only black person at his high school, graduated from Holy Cross in 1971 in English Literature and Yale Law School in 1974, and was appointed to the U.S. Supreme Court in 1991.

Or, perhaps, people I've been privileged to know personally. Like Jeanne, sent to foster care at age 8 after her mother was committed to a mental institution, sexually abused by her father at age 12 after she had not seen or heard from him for almost 7 years, moved from foster home to foster home, where she encountered physical and sexual abuse at the hands of foster parents, and who was pregnant by age 16—yet, she nonetheless won a National Science Foundation REU (Research Experience for Undergraduates) grant for original research, which she carried out while, as throughout college, raising her daughter; she later completed her Ph.D. in neurobiology and behavior, established a publication record that warranted a tenured position as Associate Professor at a Carnegie Research I institution, pursued a successful consulting practice, engaged as an advocate with community organizations, and acquired extensive teaching experience with culturally diverse populations.

Want to call these cases "exceptions?" Go ahead, admit you don't have a clue.

Which will be true if you follow the delusions of contemporary social work practice: "Social justice is the view that everyone deserves equal economic, political and social rights and opportunities. Social workers aim to open the doors of access and opportunity for everyone, particularly those in greatest need" (National Association of Social Workers, 2104, opening statement, http://www.socialworkers.org/pressroom/features/issue/peace.asp).

"Social justice" makes for wonderfully generous sentiments. Unfortunately, the social work profession, like most people, uses this term in a culturally incomprehensible manner. The sentiments behind "social justice" resolve to "fairness," and fairness means (in addition that you not seek to kill me, which I reserve for myself) to treat me fairly by reference to the pertinent cultural norms. Advocates, characteristically, postulate that they can know, without asking, what I, or anyone other than them, counts as fair. Even more frightening, social justice advocates impute these imaginary evaluations onto arbitrarily labelled groups under the illusion that there's no such thing as cultural variation. What, precisely, counts as an open door? Access? Opportunity? Need? And that's the least of the problems.

Alternatively, think through how human minds work.

If the meaning of things comes from the assumptions we apply to them, "things" can't do things and cannot have "effects." Effects come from people who choose among options in light of the cultural postulate(s) by which they give meaning to "things." Sequences of choices use our stress mechanism to track consequences and adjust choice frames. Which explains why aggregate behavioral patterns minimize energy output and maximize the reliability of energy input (approximately) and why human history exhibits consistent improvements in how we live our lives.

Jeanne explains her rise out of poverty and violence by reference to a postulate that approximates *Life Is Tough and People Will Try to Hurt You; Deal with It*—by (h/t Galaxy Quest) acting on the moral vision *Never Give Up, Never Surrender!* She looked for opportunities, worked at them, fell down (sometimes disastrously) and got up again, accepted help when offered but never assumed it was coming—much less that it was her due. She did not grant cultural authority over her own path to others—which periodic mentors admired and encouraged, since they, too, gave cultural authority to exemplars of personal responsibility.

That's how cultures work, of course. People who share a given postulate and its moral vision encourage one another to persist in actions that correspond with that vision and offer corrections when you slip—by virtue of shared actions they form a community that works together to achieve ends individuals by themselves could not hope to reach. Without that community, you don't have a team, you'll fall flat on your face, and you'll eventually lose the strength to rise again.

Likewise, "bully" is just another word for a cultural authority who acts to correct norm violations. A person or set of people who inflicts on you physical damage *not* legitimated by one of *your* cultural authorities counts as an enemy—to whom you respond with defensive action and anger. A female bodybuilder, for example, felt stunned when a National Health Service nurse in the United Kingdom insisted that her BMI of 29 meant that she was just short of obese and should eat less and exercise more (*Mail Online*, March 26, 2014, http://www.dailymail.co.uk/news/article-2589794/Female-bodybuilder-told-diet-exercise-branded-obese-NHS-nurse.html). The nurse's conclusion, of course, rested on the authority of a culture that enshrines fixed reference points set by "experts."

The woman's current physical characteristics reflect a shift from a culture that left her overweight to a culture that pushed her to take systematic weight training and exercise seriously. Without a clear shift, the authority of a previously held culture—a nurse—claiming that she was obese or close to it might have induced pain. In Anita's case, the authority of her new culture meant that she responded with anger to warn others of the dangers they might face if they relied on the authority of BMI "experts."

Who counts as a bully? A person or a set of people who inflict on you physical or emotional damage legitimated by one of your cultural authorities—to whom (therefore) you respond with embarrassment and a sense of failure—which may kill you, of course (Chapter 6), via emotional damage, far quicker than the physical damage that may have been inflicted. Bullys thus cannot exist unless you give them the authority to hurt you.

Similarly, one person cannot rape another. "Rape" like bullying rests on a specific cultural assumption that, if you take for granted an alternative cultural assumption—like, say, the Dyak in the Indonesian Borneo community of Gerai, on whom Christine Helliwell reports (2000)—it becomes absurd to think that, other than for children for whom forced entry tears and scars, a penis might hurt you. "Rape," as understood in a culture widely shared in the United States, cannot exist. However, there remains the possibility that a rape culture pervades the United States. I've never seen it described, however—even by many of my former graduate students who wrote Ph.D. dissertations based on extensive study of topics closely related, if not precisely, to sexual abuse of one kind or another.

As indicated in Chapter 3, "rapes" may occur without anyone doing anything wrong. It's common, for example, to equate sexual assault with violence, threats, and so forth. But what counts as a threat? Sexual assault literature now encompasses men as well as women and reveals that it counts as a "threat" when your girlfriend says she won't go out with you again unless you have sex with her. Is it "violence" to initiate activities that may lead to sex and to persist in the face of resistance—or is it a way to demonstrate the confidence a real man should display? Or is it a way to demonstrate the genuine interest of a woman who, because she takes for granted that solid relationships must rest on open and honest behavior, rejects coy or teasing behavior? To complicate matters, as Hanna Rosin reports in her article "When Men Are Raped" (2014), new data suggest that "men are often the victims of sexual assault, and women are often the perpetrators."

And, lest a silly person reads into these words his or her own fantasies: please dismiss the argument that you make yourself a victim when you think of yourself as a victim. Human minds don't work that way. To reiterate: when you imagine that you act on your own volition, remember that you're hearing your Interpreter try to make sense of some experience. I, and you, respond emotionally by reference to our cultures and, via cultural authorities, our sense of fairness. Talk therapy aims (albeit unrecognized by most therapists) to help a person with emotional damage shift cultures. Danielle Wozniak, currently Director, School of Social Work, University of New England, may have produced the most successful culture-based therapy procedures to date (see her, with Karen Allen, 2013 book *Surviving Domestic Violence*). More generally, if you're of the *My Culture Made Me Do It* persuasion, please *(dramatic eyes-rolling-back-in-head). Of course* your culture made you do it. That's what cultures do.

Cultures do things, however, only when team behavior corresponds to its moral vision (more or less). Cultural effectiveness depends on the degree of correspondence. Cultures-as-teams succeeded and grew increasingly successful by selecting for a mind that produces new things and a series of cognitive biases that produce the clarity necessary for making a behavioral choice and that emotionally loads experiences to direct our attention to achievements and mistakes and by requiring us to give great weight to cultural authority, to force compliance with a specific moral vision. You know cultural authorities as the cast of characters and the voices in your head that tell you what's best to do and who praises you for doing so.

And that's only part of the story. Do not forget that one small area in which individuals exercise agency, leaping from one culture to another. Sequences of choices respond to consequences, adjust, and create improved cultural designs. Cultures can kill us. Cultures take us to destinations for which they were designed. If you want to go elsewhere, pick a new culture, one that will take you there. We're here only because our mind also evolved another bias that, in the presence of evolutionarily significant threats, tells us to change assumptions and act according to another moral vision—to create or shift to a better alternative. Other cultures can kill us, too—or damage us badly if they don't. Camille Paglia reminds us: "Misled by the naive optimism and 'You go, girl!' boosterism of their upbringing, young women do not see the animal eyes glowing at them in the dark" (http://time.com/3444749/camille-paglia-the-modern-campus-cannot-comprehend-evil/).

And if your culture makes you try to treat me unfairly—rape me, batter me, threaten my grandchildren, destroy people I hold dear, whatever—my culture will make me stop you, violently if appropriate. Deal with it.

Unexamined Postulates—Distinguish What's Real from What's Not

It's tough to do so. Evolved cognitive processes make it very easy for you to act according to cultural expectations and very hard to go against those norms. The assumptions that produce those norms-rules-expectations remain inaccessible—you must work hard to make them explicit, which mostly takes too much effort and, perhaps, skills you don't have. Without critical analysis of the assumptions on which our moral visions rest, we remain oblivious, perhaps to our detriment. Too often the result produces a form of wishful thinking that may clarify our choices but that may elicit disaster—for example, new gun-control legislation passed recently by the Connecticut Legislature (supposedly the "toughest gun laws in the nation"), which the governor signed into law.

Whoever came up with "toughest gun laws in the nation" possesses an extraordinary sense of irony. Nothing in this legislation protects our children from another Sandy Hook massacre. To the contrary, they create the possibility that Connecticut will morph into a state version of Chicago, whose streets run red with blood despite gun bans and ammunition sales restrictions.

First, most components of the law can be enforced only after the fact and thus do nothing to prevent violence. Like all those who went before, the person who murders the next set of children won't be on the Dangerous Weapon Offender Registry list until after he, or she, massacres. Universal Background Check violations can't be known until someone kills with a firearm they received illegally—which is how the people who inflict by far the most gun violence get their guns now and will continue to do. In the meanwhile, the State of Connecticut has no means to detect widespread civil disobedience regarding large-capacity magazine registration, or newly acquired large-capacity magazines, or firearms safe storage, or acquisition of ammunition without an eligibility certificate. Unless, of course, the disobedient publicize their actions to shame politicians.

Second, provisions that may be enforceable still do nothing to protect our children. The expanded assault weapons ban rests on the fantasy that the functional capabilities of this imaginary category of threat is not already readily duplicated by a very large range of semiautomatic, and pump- and lever-action, rifles. Like the classic Winchester Model 1894, which as manufactured by Winchester, Marlin, and Rossi, among others, remains popular into the 21st century. The ban on large- capacity magazines rests on the fantasy that magazine capacity bears on killing potential. Even 5- round magazines allow reloads fast enough to kill 5 people every 10–15 seconds with aimed shots. Four 15-second intervals occur every minute, enough time to kill 20 people. In the 11 minutes or so Adam Lanza took to begin and end shooting in Newtown, killing 26, an experienced shooter with 5-round magazines could kill 220 people or more. A bumbling shooter who takes a full 30 seconds to reload would kill "only" 110 people over the same 11 minutes. Moreover, this ban, too, can't be enforced. Gun shops in Connecticut may have to close their doors, but gun shops in Rhode Island, New Hampshire, Vermont, Maine, and Pennsylvania can look forward to an economic boom. As can other service providers who accomplish the same end.

Elected representatives thus chose to do nothing to prevent a future mass killing. Connecticut legislators should be ashamed to leave our children at the mercy of killers. But shame requires a sense of guilt. They, like legislators in Colorado, Maryland, New York, and elsewhere, dishonored themselves and insulted their employers—us, we the people, if we are to believe the people who wrote the Constitution of the United States.

But what if the federal government enacted equivalent gun and ammunition regulations that apply everywhere?

That, of course, would violate the 2nd Amendment, which was designed (as the U.S. Supreme Court has systematically ruled) as a response to overwhelming empirical evidence—and aphorisms that range from the elegant ("Power corrupts, and absolute power corrupts absolutely"; Lord Acton) to the gritty ("A fish rots from the head"; Kru Proverb)—that governments kill and otherwise intensively exploit citizens who can't defend themselves.

Which returns us to Sowell's unconstrained and constrained visions mentioned in Chapter 3. Our finding? Both visions have merit. Human nature changes only over evolutionary, multiple- generation time spans and, for all intents and purposes, remains unchanging from one generation to another. Existing human nature is both selfish and perfectible. Which characteristic shows itself depends on exposure to consequences, or not. Recall—our minds come with a cognitive mechanism that insists that we experience fair treatment—meaning that people do not try to kill us and treat us according to our cultural norms. Consequently (pun intended), the minds of people who experience no consequences for a specific act tell them that they are entitled to do so again anytime and anyplace. The minds of people who experience consequences for a specific act tell them that they violated another's sense of fairness and that they should correct their behavior.

Current school safety policies across much of the United States rest on the (unconstrained) cultural postulate that people are naturally good but, being human, make mistakes. This cultural assumption yields the moral precept that you should teach people to be good and should help norm violators restore their innate good selves. The norms produced by this cultural assumption don't tell us how to achieve these goals, how to know if our attempts were successful, and how we may reliably anticipate what a specific person will do. Without valid answers to questions like these, claims that new legislation improves the safety of our children must count instead as self-serving and aimless flailing and wailing that aid and abet anyone who wishes to murder our children sometime in the future. In light of our findings regarding Sowell's proposed visions, the cultural foundations of current school safety policies rest on demonstrably weak premises. It's time to change cultures. Maybe we should take seriously the abundant evidence that people will exploit you if they can and treat you well only if they must. This alternative cultural assumption yields a very different moral vision, one which tells us not to rely on wishful thinking to protect our children. One component of the new culture may be shame induced with guilty verdicts and prison time. The next time such a shooting occurs—and it will—all who voted yes or signed bills with provisions like those in Connecticut's "toughest gun laws in the nation," that endanger our children, should be prosecuted, as are others who act in furtherance of a criminal act, as accessories to murder.

Unexamined Postulates—Critical Analysis May Reveal Threats

Question Authority became a popular slogan, as I remember it, sometime in the 1960s. But its origins may date to Socrates, who warned against the logical fallacy of Appeal to Authority (*argumentum ab auctoritate*) and its complement, Appeal to the Absence of Authority, otherwise known as *argumentum ad hominem*. Socrates, like many since (including me), was interested in truth, not fantasy. And the natural operation of human minds make these errors ("clarifying" cognitive biases) extraordinarily common. Cultural authorities—the cast of characters and voices in our minds—keep up an unceasing litany of what we should do and heap praise on us when we do so. And invective when we stray. Particularly when we stray and give credence to authorities from other cultures. Either case poses great danger.

Norms rest on postulates, and postulates may rest on nothing more than fantasy, which explains why critical analysis focuses on postulates. Assumptions, by definition, defy "proof." But assumptions have implications, and we may test implications to assess the usefulness of the assumptions on which they rest. Critical assessment of postulates thus may uncover threats, subtle rather than dramatic but threats nonetheless.

You may realize that one of your cultures won't take you where you want to go. Find yourself incarcerated and want out? Change cultures. In danger of incarceration (likely recognized by your mother, other family member, or someone who thinks you show promise)? Change cultures. It doesn't take a miracle to escape poverty and drugs. But it does take the right culture. Ask Wes Moore. The other Wes Moore, also growing up, only blocks away, in poverty without a father amid crime and drugs in Baltimore, had only his older brother to provide effective guidance. Both Moores lived up to the expectations of their cultural authorities. One became a Rhodes Scholar, an Afghanistan veteran, entrepreneur, and (among other things) a special assistant to Condoleeza Rice. The other found himself incarcerated with a life sentence.

Ragashanti—as he's known to most people—became one of my Ph.D. students on a path he found himself traveling after he, too, changed cultures. Growing up in Kingston, Jamaica, and involved like both Wes Moores with drugs and crime, Ragashanti switched cultures and received a B.A. degree from Vassar College and a Ph.D. from University of Connecticut. He taught at the University of the West Indies (Mona) until he followed his passion into the entertainment industry. How'd this happen? Start with a redefinition of success. When he was 19, Ragashanti found himself in jail for the third time. His sense that a life on the streets supported by illegal activities, which "real men" undertook because they were victimized by white people and uptown people, might turn out to be a dead end that would soon kill him. Add memories of his mother telling him that he "have the brain," a teacher praising him as very promising and bright, and a prominent lawyer retained by the teacher who stated the message clearly: "People believe in you. Time for you to believe in yourself." Take a different path, starting with a change of assumptions. Abandon the one that blamed others for your life circumstances. Adopt the one that placed responsibility for your life circumstances on you. This change in cultural assumptions meant a new moral vision. School, like all life experiences, was no longer something you should expect to improve your life. On the contrary, the new moral vision told Ragashanti that he should take experiences of all kinds—from sweeping the floor, to collecting empty bottles off the street for small change, to school—and make them work for him.

Did he excel in school, get into Vassar, earn a Ph.D., teach at the University of the West Indies, and create an entertainment career on his own? Of course not. He had family and friends and many mentors along the way. That's what teams are for, of course. And that's how teams' strength achieves ends we'd otherwise miss.

To reiterate—cultures aren't merely the things other people think and do, and culture change means dramatically more than changing how a person thinks and acts. Culture change means to change *teams*, thus to change the supportive communities of people who share the postulates that rationalize the moral vision that will take you where you want to go. Want to avoid or escape domestic violence? Change your culture, join another team. As Susan DiVietro writes: "At the end of a very long, very painful interview recounting the horrific details of abuse at the hands of her then ex-husband, I reached what I considered the most interesting question on my interview protocol. 'What do you think would have made a difference? What would have helped?' Without hesitation, 'A friend,' she said. 'It would have helped if I had a friend. Even just one friend' "(2010, xx).

Fall in love with the wrong person? The Middle Eastern/South Asian honor culture community will kill you. An honor culture community that takes for granted that its job is to protect one another will keep you safe. That same culture will minimize your chance of being gang raped at a fraternity party and will act to enforce consequences to destroy the genuine rape culture that entraps others—check Peggy Sanday's 1990 Fraternity Gang Rape.

Unexamined Postulates—Another Way to Say Cultural Incompetence

Prevailing ways to think about issues like these frame them correctly as forms of conflict but wrongly as things that occur between individuals. Sometimes, people count as the supposed conflict agents. At other times, organizations or states count as the conflict agents.

Proposed solutions resolve themselves into one or another version of "change how people (slash-organizations-slash-states) think about the issues." Proposals like these reliably fail, because they fail to address problem origins in the postulates that produce the moral vision that people's minds tell them to enact. More than 80 Branch Davidian members were killed in 1993 in choices attributable directly to the cultural incompetence of federal agents from the ATF and FBI. Malcolm Gladwell's (2014) *New Yorker* article "Sacred and Profane" summarizes the issues clearly; but also read survivor Clive Doyle's (2012) memoir *Journey to Waco*. Gladwell highlights the central cultural incompetence question when he observed that "the question Doyle poses in his memoir, with genuine puzzlement, is how a religious community could go to such lengths to explain itself to such little effect." The answer? The extraordinarily difficult task of questioning our cultural authorities and taking seriously the moral vision of another cultural authority. The FBI defined the Branch Davidians at Mount Carmel Center in Waco as hostages and David Koresh as their captor. Mount Carmel residents defined themselves free to come and go as they wished but also as "living through the 'fifth seal'—a late stage in the end of time, during which believers are asked to suffer through a round of bloodshed, to 'wait a little season,' and then to suffer a second round." Biblical scholars James Tabor and Phillip Arnold recognized the postulate on which the Davidians had built their moral vision, approached the FBI, and produced an alternative interpretation of the Book of Revelation, and sent it to Koresh—who, Gladwell notes, wrote back: "I am presently being permitted to document in structured form the decoded messages of the seven seals." "Upon the completion of this task, I will be freed of my waiting period. . . . As soon as I can see that people like Jim Tabor and Phil Arnold have a copy, I will come out and then you can do your thing with this beast."

The Feds didn't wait. They assumed that Koresh could not be trusted. That assumption ruled out the possibility that he might make truthful statements; 76 people soon died—exemplar of cultural incompetence.

Minds unthreatened by other people's specific acts incorporate those actions into their own repertoire (the chameleon effect). Minds threatened by other people's specific acts—finding them, for example, unpredictable/confusing/and so on—avoid the chameleon effect and maintain cultural differences. Until you learn to identify the postulate that produces a given moral vision, you guarantee conflict and dismiss any chance of conflict resolution. Untold damage occurs daily as people hurl righteous words at each other. It may be time to take seriously the slogan Question Authority. Particularly, question your own cultural authorities, who assert one claim and denigrate contrary claims. Require evidence.

Unexamined Postulates—Conflict Resolution Calls for Cultural Convergence

Clashing cultures resolve unsurprisingly, as mentioned a few paragraphs earlier, to: "If your culture makes you try to treat me unfairly—rape me, batter me, threaten my grandchildren, destroy people I hold dear, whatever—my culture will make me stop you, violently if appropriate." Conflict analysis lays bare multiple levels of complexity to any given conflict. Beyond the obvious—conflicting moral visions—there lies (nearly as obvious) the postulates that produce those visions. Beyond those cultural differences there lies (mostly now hidden) the multiple cultures that bear on a conflict; beyond the immediate conflict, complicating clashes may be implicit in cultures that bear on how you should respond to norm violations, or how you can know the content of another person's culture. Nonviolence resolutions, however, assume cultural convergence. Here's an exercise to help clarify the issue: racist or not?

For simplicity, let's assume Dr. M. L. King Jr.'s distinctions between racist and nonracist cultures:

- Racist culture (of whatever kind) postulates that skin color (the primary marker for "race") signals a fundamental difference in kind between groups. (Note that *any* physical characteristic may substitute, with the same effect—for example, gender, height, ethnicity, weight, disability, or pick-your-own-feature). Racist cultural norms/rules/expectations tell you (among other things) that variation in your evaluations of people and what they do should correspond with their race.
- Nonracist culture (of whatever kind) assumes no fundamental difference in kind between groups—whether marked by skin color, gender, height, ethnicity, weight, disability, or some other physical characteristic. Hence (among other things) variation in your evaluations of people and what they do should not correspond with some physical characteristic but, instead, with some behavioral characteristic, which reflects the moral visions of one or another culture.

"Race" or its equivalent makes its way without letup into the narratives of everyday life. In 2012–2014, events pertaining to Trayvon Martin, George Zimmerman, and Michael Brown dominated the news for months. In 2006, Crystal Mangum, Duke University Faculty, Duke Lacrosse team members, and prosecutor Mike Nifong dominated the news in very much the same way. Read all you can about either case. Or, pick another issue or set of cases—maybe involving sexism, or immigration, or disability. Look over the commentary on these cases, apply the criteria that differentiate racist and nonracist cultures to distinguish racist commentary and behavior from nonracist commentary and behavior. In short, ask two simple questions:

- If you act on the moral vision of a racist culture, which commentary and which behavior (including written commentary) should you produce?
- If you act on the moral vision of a nonracist culture, which commentary and which behavior (including written commentary) should you produce?

For example, and more recently, was Kobe Bryant wrong to refuse to react one way or another just because he was "African-American" and, if so (as Jim Brown charged), why? What postulate rationalizes that norm/expectation/rule? Is it the view that my UConn political science colleague Shayla Nunnally reports that many "black" parents teach their children that "whites" count as their enemy? Does an equivalent speculation rationalize tension, sometimes outright hostility, between people with the same shade of skin but with cultures that vary corresponding with (say) birth in New York City instead of Kingston, Jamaica, or Accra, Ghana? Can you "act white" without thinking of yourself as "black?" If you think of yourself as "black," does "acting white" mean selling out or buying in? Who cares about variations in skin shade—and why? And, if you do, doesn't that make you racist?

Then, assemble and report evidence that the assumptions on which racist and non-racist cultures rest are valid.

Do so likewise with evidence bearing on the empirical validity of the postulates of overlapping cultures—like those that may tell you how you should respond to norm violations and those that may require you to ask people about what goes on in their minds or assure you that you need not ask. You may find yourself following a culture based on a false premise. If so, you'll make more satisfying choices if you change cultures. The process offers the prospect of conflict resolution, if your choices exhibit the cultural convergence we've called the *chameleon effect*. The alternative? Choices framed as losses, not gains, and violence.

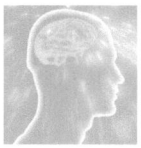

References

Armony, J. L., and LeDoux, J. E. (1997) How the brain processes emotional information. *Annals, New York Academy of Sciences*: 259–70.
Arnsten, A. F. T. (1998) The biology of being frazzled. *Science* 280: 1711–12.
Barkow J. H., Cosmides, L., & Tooby, J. (Eds.) (1992) *The Adapted Mind: Evolutionary Psychology and the Generation of Culture*. New York: Oxford University Press.
Barnett, H. G. (1953) *Innovation: The basis of Cultural Change*. New York: McGraw-Hill.
———. (1965). Laws of socio-cultural change. *International Journal of Comparative Sociology* 6: 207–30.
Bartlett, F. C. (1932) *Remembering*. New York: Cambridge University Press.
Bastian, B., Denson, T. F., and Haslam, N. (2013) The roles of dehumanization and moral outrage in retributive justice. *PloS One* 8: e61842; Doi: 0.1371/journal.pone.0061842.
Bauer, P. (1954) *West African Trade: A Study of Competition, Oligopoly and Monopoly in a Changing Economy*. New York: Cambridge University Press.
Berg, E. (1968) Socialist ideology and marketing policy in Africa. In R. Moyer and S. C. Hollander, Eds., *Markets and Marketing in Developing Economies*, pp. 24–47. Homewood, IL: Irwin.
Bernard, H. R., Killworth, P. D. (1973) On the social structure of an ocean-going research vessel and other important things. *Social Science Research* 2:145–84.
Berns, G. S., Cohen, J. D., and Mintun, M. A. (1998) Brain regions responsive to novelty in the absence of awareness. *Science* 280: 1272–75.
Bowles, S., and Gintis, H. (2011). *A Cooperative Species: Human Reciprocity and Its Evolution*. Princeton, NJ: Princeton University Press.
Boyd, R., & Richerson, P. (1985) *Culture and the Evolutionary Process*. Chicago: University of Chicago Press.
Brewer, J. B., et al. (1998) Making memories: Brain activity that predicts how well visual experience will be remembered. *Science* 281:1185–87.

Bueno de Mesquita, B. (2003) Ruminations on challenges to prediction with rational choice models. *Rationality and Society* 15: 136–47.
Bueno de Mesquita, B., & McDermott, R. (2004) Crossing no man's land: Cooperation from the trenches. *Political Psychology* 25: 271–87.
Calvin, W. H. (1996) *The Cerebral Code: Thinking a Thought in the Mosaics of the Mind.* Cambridge, MA: MIT Press.
Centers for Disease Control (CDC) (2003) *Costs of Intimate Partner Violence against Women in the United States.* Atlanta, GA.
Cottrol, R. J., Diamond, R. T. (1991) The Second Amendment: Toward an Afro-Americanist reconsideration. *Georgetown Law Journal* 80: 309–61.
D'Andrade, R. (2002) Cultural Darwinism and language. *American Anthropologist* 104: 223–32.
De Martino, B., Kumaran, D., Semour, B., & Dolan, R. J. (2006) Frames, biases, and rational decision making in the human brain. *Science* 313: 684–87.
De Quervain, D. F.-J., et al. (2004) The neural basis of altruistic punishment. *Science* 305: 1254–58.
DiVietro, S. C. (2010) *"Sanctions and Sanctuary" Revisited: Domestic Violence and Cultural Models of Intervention.* Ph.D. dissertation, paper AAI3464338, http://digitalcommons.uconn.edu/dissertations/AAI3464338.
Douglass, F. (1845) *Narrative of the Life of Frederick Douglass, an American Slave,* https://archive.org/details/oates71026420.
Doyle, C. (2012) *Journey to Waco.* Lanham, MD: Rowman & Littlefield.
Easton, D. (1953) *The Political System: An Inquiry into the State of Political Science.* New York: Knopf.
French, B. H., Tilghman, J. D., and Malabranche, D. A. (2014) Sexual coercion context and psychosocial correlates among diverse males. *Psychology of Men and Masculinity,* http://dx.doi.org/10.1037/a0035915.
Fuentes, C. (2008) Pathways from interpersonal violence to sexually transmitted infections: A mixed-method study of diverse women. *Journal of Women's Health* 17: 1591–1603.
Gazzaniga, M. (1988) *The Mind's Past.* Berkeley and Los Angeles: University of California Press.
Geertz, C. (1962) The growth of culture and the evolution of mind. In J. Sher (Ed.), *Theories of the Mind,* pp. 713–40. New York: Free Press
Gilens, M., and Page, B. I. (2014) Testing theories of American politics: Elites, interest groups, and average citizens, *Perspectives on Politics.*
Gius, M. (2014) An examination of the effects of concealed weapons laws and assault weapons bans on state-level murder rates. *Applied Economics Letters* 21: 265–67, http://dx.doi.org/10.1080/13504851.2013.854294.
Gladwell, M. (2014) Sacred and profane: How not to negotiate with believers. *The New Yorker,* March 31.
Glimcher, P. W., Dorris, M. C., and Bayer, H. M. (2005) Physiological utility theory and the neuroeconomics of choice. *Games and Economic Behavior* 52(2): 213–56.
Green, E. (2011) *Broken Promises.* Sausalito, CA: PoliPointPress.
Grossman, D. (2009) *On Killing* (rev. ed.). Boston: Little, Brown & Co.
Hahn, R. A., Bilukha, O. O., Crosby, A., Fullilove, M. T., et al. (2003) *First Reports Evaluating the Effectiveness of Strategies for Preventing Violence: Firearms Laws.* Findings from the Task Force on Community Preventative Services. Atlanta: Centers for Disease Control and Prevention.

Halbrook, S. P. (2013) *Gun Control in the Third Reich: Disarming the Jews and "Enemies of the State."* Oakland, CA: Independent Institute.
Handwerker, W. P. (1987) Fiscal corruption and the moral economy of resource acquisition. *Research in Economic Anthropology* 9: 307–53.
———. (1989a) The origins and evolution of culture. *American Anthropologist* 91, 313–26.
———. (1989b). *Women's Power and Social Revolution: Fertility Transition in West Indies.* Newbury Park, CA: Sage.
———. (1993) Gender power differences between parents and high risk sexual behavior: AIDS/STD risk factors extend to a prior generation. *Journal of Women's Health* 2: 301–16.
———. (1996) Power and gender: Violence and affection experienced by children in Barbados. *Medical Anthropology* 17: 101–28.
———. (1998) Why violence? *Human Organization* 57: 200–08.
———. (1999) Childhood origins of depression: Evidence from native and nonnative women in Alaska and the Russian Far East. *Journal of Women's Health* 8: 87–94.
———. (2001) Child abuse and the balance of power in parental relationships: An evolved domain-independent mental mechanism that accounts for behavioral variation. *American Journal of Human Biology* 13: 679–89.
———. (2003) Traumatic stress, ecological contingency, and sexual behavior: Antecedents and consequences of sexual precociousness, sexual mobility, and childbearing in adolescence. *Ethos* 31: 385–411.
———. (2009) *The Origin of Cultures.* Walnut Creek, CA: Left Coast Press.
Haney, C., Banks, C., and Zimbardo, P. (1973) A study of prisoners and guards in a simulated prison. *Naval Research Review*: 1–17.
Harris, S. (2011) *The Truth about Violence*, Nov. 5, http://m.samharris.org/blog/item/the-truth-about-violence.
———. (2013) The Riddle of the Gun, January 2, http://m.samharris.org/blog/item/the-riddle-of-the-gun/.
Harvey, J. B. (1974) The Abilene paradox and other meditations on management. *Organizational Dynamics* 3: 63–80.
Hayden, B. (1995) *Archaeology.* New York: W. H. Freeman.
Helliwell, C. (2000) "It's only a penis": Rape, feminism, and difference. *Signs: Journal of Women in Culture and Society* 25(3): 789–816.
Henrich, J., and Henrich, N. (2006) Culture, evolution, and the puzzle of human cooperation. *Cognitive Systems Research* 7: 220–45.
Henrich J., McElreath, R., Barr, A., Ensminger, J., et al. (2006) Costly punishment across human societies. *Science* 312: 1767–70.
Hobbes, T. (1651) *Leviathan,* https://archive.org/details/hobbessleviathan00hobbuoft.
Hoebel, E. A. (1954) *The Law of Primitive Man.* Cambridge, MA: Harvard University Press.
Huth, P. K. (1999) Deterrence and international conflict: Empirical findings and theoretical debates. *American Review of Political Science* 2: 25–48.
Israeli R. A. (2002) Manual of Islamic fundamentalist terrorism. *Terrorism and Political Violence* 14: 23–40.
Jerison, H. J. (1973). *Evolution of the Brain and Intelligence.* New York: Academic Press.
Johnson, N. (2014) *Negros and the Gun: The Black Tradition of Arms.* Amherst, NY: Prometheus Books.
Jones, R. (1991) The Political and Economic Dynamics of Sexual Diseases. Paper delivered to the annual meetings of the American Anthropological Association (Chicago).

Jorgensen, J. G. (1990) *Oil Age Eskimos*. Berkeley and Los Angeles: University of California Press.

Jorgensen, J. G., McCleary, R., and McNabb, S. (1985) Social indicators in Alaskan Native villages. *Human Organization* 44: 2–17.

Junger, S. (2010) *War*. New York: Hatchette Book Group.

Kahneman, D. (2003) Maps of bounded rationality: Psychology for behavioral economics. *The American Economic Review* 93: 1449–75.

Kahneman, D., & Tversky, A. (1979) Prospect theory. *Econometrica* 47: 263–92.

Kates, D. B. (1992) The Second Amendment and the ideology of self-protection. *Constitutional Commentary* 9: 87–104.

Kates, D. B., Schaffer, H. E., Lattimer, J. K., Murray, G. B., and Cassem, E. H. (1994) Guns and public health. *Tennessee Law Review* 62: 513–96.

Kleck, G., and Gertz, M. (1995) Armed resistance to crime: The prevalence and nature of self-defense with a gun. *The Journal of Criminal Law and Criminology* 86: 150–87.

Kleck, G., Sever, B., Li, S., and Gertz, M. (2005) The missing link in general deterrence research. *Criminology* 43: 623–59.

Kopel, D. B. (2004a) The Torah and self-defense. *Penn State Law Review* 109:17–42.

———. (2004b) The Scottish and English religious roots of the American right to arms. *Bridges* 12: 291–312.

———. (2006) Self-defense in Asian religions. *Journal of Firearms and Public Policy* 18.

Kopel, D. B., Gallan, P., and Eisen, J. D. (2006) Is resisting genocide a human right? *Notre Dame Law Review* 81.

Kotkin, J. (2014a) Dawn of the Age of Oligarchy: The alliance between government and the 1%, *The Daily Beast*, http://www.joelkotkin.com/content/00924-dawn-age-oligarchy-alliance-between-government-and-1.

———. (2014b) Watch what you say, June 7th, *New Geography*, http://www.newgeography.com/content/004355-watch-what-you-say-the-new-liberal-power-elite-won-t-tolerate-dissent.

Kraus, R. F., and Buffler, P. A. (1979) Sociocultural stress and the American Native in Alaska. *Culture, Medicine, and Psychiatry* 3: 111–51.

Kroeber, A. L. (1917) The superorganic. *American Anthropologist* 19: 163–213.

Kroeber, A. L., and Kluckhohn, C. (1952) *Culture: A Critical Review of Concepts and Definitions*. New York: Vintage Books.

Lasswell, H. (1936) *Politics: Who Gets What When and How*, http://www.policysciences.org/classics/politics.pdf.

Lee, R. B., and DeVore, I. (Eds.) 1968 *Man the Hunter*. Chicago: Aldine.

Leef, G. (2014) Party schools: Years of fun mostly at other people's expense, but not much learning, March 7, *Forbes*, http://www.forbes.com/sites/georgeleef/2014/03/07/party-schools-years-of-fun-mostly-at-other-peoples-expense-but-not-much-learning/.

Lehrer, J. (2011) How power corrupts, May 18, *Wired*, http://archive.wired.com/wiredscience/2011/05/how-power-corrupts/.

Linton, R. (1936) *The Study of Man*. New York: Appleton Century Crofts.

Lott, J. R. Jr. (2010) *More Guns, Less Crime* (3rd ed.). Chicago: University of Chicago Press.

Machiavelli, N. (1950). *The Prince*. New York: Random House.

Marris, P., and Somerset, A. (1971) *African Businessmen: A Study of Entrepreneurship and Development in Kenya*, p. 197. London: Routledge & Kegan Paul.

McGaugh J. (1989) Involvement of hormonal and neuromodulatory systems in the regulation of memory storage. *Annual Review of Neuroscience* 12: 255.

McNabb, S. (1990) Native health status and Native health policy: Current dilemmas at the federal levels. *Arctic Anthropology* 27: 2–35.
Milgram, S. (1963). Behavioral study of obedience. *Journal of Abnormal Psychology* 67: 371–78.
———. (1974) *Obedience to Authority: An Experimental View.* New York: Harper & Row.
Mlot, C. (1998) Probing the biology of emotion. *Science* 280: 1005–07.
Muller, H. (1952) *The Uses of the Past.* New York: Oxford University Press.
Nairne J. S., Thompson, S. R., and Pandeirada, J. N. S. (2007) Adaptive memory: Survival processing enhances retention. *Journal of Experimental Psychology: Learning, Memory, and Cognition.* 33: 263–73.
National Research Council (1989) *Arctic Social Science: An Agenda for Action.* Washington, D.C.: National Academy Press.
Nunnally, S. C. (2010) Learning race, socializing blackness. *Du Bois Review* 7: 185–217.
Osofsky, M. J., Bandura, A., and Zimbardo, P. G. (2005) The role of moral disengagement in the execution process. *Law and Human Behavior* 29: 371–93.
Paine, P. (2014) Rape culture theory ensnares innocent men, *Legal Insurrection*, June 30, http://legalinsurrection.com/2014/06/rape-culture-theory-ensnares-innocent-men/.
Plutchik, R. (1980). *Theories of Emotion.* New York: Academic Press.
Pollan, M. (2013) The intelligent plant, December 23, *The New Yorker*.
Polsby, D. D., and Kates, D. B. (2004) Of holocausts and gun control. *Washington University Law Quarterly* 75: 1237.
Pynoos, R. S. , Steinberg, A. M., Ornitz, E. M., and Goenjian, A. K. (1997) Issues in the developmental neurobiology of traumatic stress. *Annals of the New York Academy of Sciences* 821: 176–93.
Qutb, S. (1964) *Milestones (Ma'alim 'ala Al-Tariq).* Islamic Book Service; 1981 (rev. ed.) Unity Press; http://www.izharudeen.com/uploads/4/1/2/2/4122615/milestones_www.izharudeen.com.pdf.
Raphaeli, N. (2002) Ayman Muhammad Rabi' Al-Zawahiri: The making of an arch terrorist. *Terrorism and Political Violence* 14: 1–22.
Rees, G., Frith, C. D., and Lavie, N. (1997) Modulating irrelevant motion perception by varying attentional load in an unrelated task. *Science* 278: 1616–19.
Richards, B. (1994) *From Respect to Rights to Entitlement: Blocked Aspirations and Suicidal Behavior.* Paper delivered to the annual meeting of the Society for Applied Anthropology (Albuquerque).
Roozendaal B., Quirarte, G. L., and McGaugh, J. L. (1997) Stress-activated hormonal systems and the regulation of memory storage. *Annals, New York Academy of Sciences*: 247–58.
Rosin, H. (2014) When men are raped. *Slate*, April 29, http://www.slate.com/articles/double_x/doublex/2014/04/male_rape_in_america_a_new_study_reveals_that_men_are_sexually_assaulted.html.
Rousseau, J.-J. (1762) *The Social Contract.* http://www.constitution.org/jjr/socon.htm.
Rugg, M. D. (1998) Memories are made of this. *Science* 281: 1151–52.
Rummel, R. J. (1994). *Death by Government.* New Brunswick, NJ: Transaction Publishers.
———. (1995) Democracy, power, genocide, and mass murder. *Journal of Conflict Resolution* 39: 3–26.
———. (1998). *Statistics of Democide: Genocide and Mass Murder since 1900.* Berlin: LIT Verlag.
Schacter, D. L. (1998) Memory and awareness. *Science* 280: 59–60.

Schwartz, S. H. (2006) Value orientations: Measurement, antecedents, and consequences across nations. In R. Jowell, C. Roberts, R. Fitzgerald, & G. Eva (Eds.), *Measuring Attitudes Cross-Nationally: Lessons from the European Social Survey*. London: Sage.
Searle, J. R. (1995) *The Construction of Social Reality*. New York: Free Press.
Selye, H. (1956). *The Stress of Life*. New York: McGraw-Hill.
Service, E. R. (1975) *Origins of the State and Civilization*. New York: Norton.
Shafir, E., & LeBoeuf. R. A. (2002) Rationality. *Annual Review of Psychology* 53: 491–517.
Sharp, L. (1952) Steel axes for stone age Australians. *Human Organization* 11: 17–22.
Smith, A. (1776) *An Inquiry into the Nature and Causes of the Wealth of Nations*. Dublin: Printed for Messrs. Whitestone.
Sosis, R., and Alcorta, C. (2008) Militants and martyrs: Evolutionary perspectives on religion and terrorism . In R. Sagarin and T. Taylor (Eds.), *Natural Security: A Darwinian Approach to a Dangerous World*, pp. 105–24. Berkeley and Los Angeles: University of California Press.
Sosis, R., and Handwerker, W. P. (2011) Psalms and coping with uncertainty: Religious Israeli women's responses to the 2006 Lebanon War. *American Anthropologist* 113: 40–55
Sowell, T. ([1987] 2007) *A Conflict of Visions*. New York: Basic Books.
———. (2000) *A Personal Odyssey*. New York: Free Press.
Steward, J. (1936) The economic and social basis of primitive bands. In *Essays on Anthropology in Honor of Alfred L. Kroeber*. Berkeley and Los Angeles: University of California Press.
Sun Tzu (2005) *The Art of Aar by Sun Tzu—Special Edition*, L. Giles (trans.). El Paso: Norte Press.
Tark, J., and Kleck, G. (2004) Resisting crime: The effect of victim action on the outcomes of crime. *Criminology* 42: 861–909.
Tett, G. (2009) *Fool's Gold*. New York: Simon & Schuster.
Thomas, C. (2007) *My Grandfather's Son*. New York: HarperCollins.
Tylor, E. (1871) *Primitive Culture*. New York: J. P. Putnam's Sons.
Wagner, A. D., et al. (1998) Building memories: Remembering and forgetting of verbal experiences as predicted by brain activity. *Science* 281: 1188–91
Wallace, A. F. C. (1970) *Culture and Personality* (2nd ed.). New York: Random House.
Watkins, T. (2009) The Contrived Nature of the Current Recession, http://www.sjsu.edu/faculty/watkins/contrivedrec.htm.
Weber, M. ([1922] 1946) *Wirtschaft und Gesellschaft*. Reprinted in translation in H. H. Gerth and C. W. Mills (Eds.), *From Max Weber: Essays in Sociology*, pp. 180–97. New York: Oxford University Press.
White, L. A. (1949) *The Science of Culture*. New York: Grove.
Wickelgren, I. (1997) Getting the brain's attention. *Science* 278: 35–37.
Wozniak, D. F., and Allen, K. (2013) *Surviving Domestic Violence: A Guide to Healing Your Soul and Building Your Future*. Avon, MA: Adams Media.
Zimbardo, P. G., Haney, C., Banks, W. C., and Jaffe, D. (1973) The mind is a formidable jailer: A Pirandellian prison. *New York Times Magazine*, April 8: 38–60.

Index

agent, agency, 5, 10-12, 17, 21, 60, 71, 79, 97-98, 114
choices, choice, choice frame, decision 9-10, 12, 17-21, 25, 28, 39, 45-46, 49, 51, 53, 55, 64-65, 69, 73-78, 80, 84, 92-93, 95-100, 102-103, 106-107, 110-111, 114, 118, 120
cognitive mechanisms, cognitive bias, 9-10, 12, 20-21, 26, 33, 50-51, 56, 72-81, 83, 85, 87, 89, 91-92, 95-96, 103, 111, 114, 116
consequences, 17, 55-57, 72, 75-79, 87, 92, 95-97, 100, 102-103, 106, 111, 114, 116
dental, dentist, 36, 47-49, 80, 82,
emotional, emotions, 10, 20, 25, 34-35, 51-52, 72, 75-77, 80, 85, 92, 101, 104, 113-114
equality, 19, 96-97, 103,
error, mistake, 20, 28, 30-32, 36, 45, 55, 57-58, 67, 71, 73-75, 92, 114, 116
evolved, evolutionary, 10, 12, 20-21, 28-29, 32-33, 47, 55, 57, 73, 74, 91-93, 95-96, 97, 100, 102-103, 106, 109, 114, 116
exploitation, 74, 77, 85, 97-98, 101-103
fair, 20, 80-82, 91-98, 101-103, 111, 113-114, 116, 119
free, 17-20, 46, 53, 62, 65, 77, 85, 101-102, 110, 118-119
intelligence, 10, 12, 18, 20, 23, 29, 30, 32, 34-35, 69, 91-93, 95,
language, 10, 12-13, 25, 42, 67-69, 79, 110
learned helplessness, 59, 73, 90-91, 95
learning, 11-12, 104-105, 124

moral, morality, 10, 14-15, 17, 20-21, 23, 25, 32-35, 37, 39, 41, 43-47, 49-51, 58, 60, 63-65, 67-69, 71-73, 75, 77-82, 87, 91, 93, 96, 98, 103, 110-112, 114-120
norm, rule, expectation, 10, 13-18, 20, 23, 26, 32, 39, 43, 45, 47-51, 56-60, 64-66, 71, 78, 80-82, 94-96, 98, 106-107, 110-112, 114, 116-117, 119, 120
(cultural) postulate, 10-14, 17, 20, 23, 32-36, 39, 45, 48, 58, 60, 71-73, 80-82, 93, 97, 110-112, 114, 116-120
power, 10-11, 16-19, 21, 24, 27, 41, 46-47, 51-57, 72, 77-79, 87-88, 91, 95-98, 100-102, 104, 115
rights (human), 11, 13, 23, 34, 45, 57, 58, 63, 67, 71, 81, 87-88, 101, 111
sex, sex sales, STDs, sexual cultures, sexual activity, sexual mobility, sexual abuse, 11, 20, 24, 35-39, 41, 44, 49-52, 58, 60, 66, 72, 80, 85-86, 94, 101-102, 111, 113, 120
stress, 10, 37, 53, 72-73, 76-77, 85-86, 90, 92, 110-111
suicide, 21, 81-82, 85-90, 95
survival, 15, 23, 25, 64, 79, 92, 96, 102, 106
team, teamwork, 10, 13, 16, 18, 20-21, 27, 33, 46, 60, 66, 68-69, 73, 78, 84, 87-89, 94-95, 110, 112, 114, 117-118, 120
violence, 9-10, 25, 36, 51, 55, 60, 62-63, 80-82, 86-91, 96-106, 111, 113-115, 118, 120

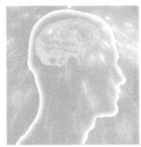

About the Author

W. Penn Handwerker, a professor of anthropology at the University of Connecticut, trained as a general anthropologist with an emphasis on the intersection of biological and cultural anthropology and has published in all five fields of anthropology (applied, archaeological, biological, cultural, and linguistic). He has done field research in West Africa, the West Indies, Russia, and various regions of the United States. He developed new methods for studying cultures while doing research on human fertility, entrepreneurship, corruption, and both inter- and intragenerational power differences. His current work extends the implications of *Our Story* to the production of quick, valid, and reliable ethnographic findings, and the critical analyses necessary for effectively Questioning Authority.